THE ANCIENT

CHINESE

= WORLD =

STUDENT STUDY GUIDE

Oxford University Press, Inc., publishes works that
further Oxford University's objective of excellence
in research, scholarship, and education.

Oxford   New York
Auckland   Cape Town   Dar es Salaam   Hong Kong   Karachi
Kuala Lumpur   Madrid   Melbourne   Mexico City   Nairobi
New Delhi   Shanghai   Taipei   Toronto

With offices in
Argentina   Austria   Brazil   Chile   Czech Republic   France   Greece
Guatemala   Hungary   Italy   Japan   Poland   Portugal   Singapore
South Korea   Switzerland   Thailand   Turkey   Ukraine   Vietnam

Published by Oxford University Press, Inc.
198 Madison Avenue, New York, New York, 10016
www.oup.com

Oxford is a registered trademark of Oxford University Press

Writer: Robert Weisser
Editor: Lelia Mander
Project Director: Jacqueline A. Ball
Education Consultant: Diane L. Brooks, Ed.D.
Design: designlabnyc

Casper Grathwohl, Publisher

Library of Congress Cataloging-in-Publication Data is available
ISBN-13: 978-0-19-522295-1 (California edition)   ISBN-13: 978-0-19-522164-0
ISBN-10: 0-19-522295-4   (California edition)   ISBN-10: 0-19-522164-8

Printing number: 9 8 7 6 5 4 3 2 1

Printed in the United States of America
on acid-free paper

Dear Parents, Guardians, and Students:

This study guide has been created to increase student enjoyment and understanding of *The Ancient Chinese World*. It has been developed in accordance with *The History–Social Science Framework for California Public Schools* to help students access the text. As they do so, they can learn history and the social sciences; improve reading, language arts, and study skills; and meet California history–social science content and analysis skills standards.

The study guide offers a wide variety of interactive exercises to support every chapter. Parents or other family members can participate in activities labeled "With a Parent or Partner." Adults can help in other ways, too. One important way is to encourage students to create and use a history journal as they work through the exercises in the guide. The journal can simply be an off-the-shelf notebook or three-ring binder used only for this purpose. Some students might like to customize their journals with markers, colored paper, drawings, or computer graphics. No matter what it looks like, a journal is a place a student's very own place to organize thoughts, practice writing, and make notes on important information. It will serve as a personal report of ongoing progress that your child's teacher can evaluate regularly. When completed, it will be a source of satisfaction and accomplishment for your child.

Sincerely,

Casper Grathwohl
Publisher

This book belongs to:

_____

CONTENTS

HOW TO USE THE STUDENT STUDY GUIDES TO
THE WORLD IN ANCIENT TIMES

The World in Ancient Times *will introduce you to some of the greatest civilizations in history, such as ancient Rome, China, and Egypt. You will read about rulers, generals, and politicians. You will learn about scientists, writers, and artists. The daily lives of these people were far different from your life today.*

The study guides to The World in Ancient Times *will help you as you read the books. They will help you learn and enjoy history while building thinking and writing skills. And they will help you meet history–social science content standards, pass important tests, and just enjoy learning. The sample pages below show the books' special features. Take a look!*

Before you read

- Have a notebook or extra paper and a pen handy to make a history journal. A dictionary and thesaurus will help you too.

- Read the two-part chapter title and predict what you will learn from the chapter.

- Quotation marks in the margin show the sources of ancient writings. The main primary sources are listed next to the chapter title.

- Study all maps and photos. Read the captions closely. (This caption tells that the statue itself is a primary source. Artifacts are records of history, just like writings.)

“ **TOMB, SARCOPHAGUS, AND STATUE FROM ROME: AULUS GELLIUS; AND LIVY**

“ Tomb from Rome, 135 BCE

“ Sarcophagus from Rome, 298 BCE

CHAPTER 5

FATHERS, GODS, AND GODDESSES
RELIGION IN ANCIENT ROME

Cornelius Scipio Hispanus was not a modest man. He praised not only himself, but his whole family as well. When he died around 135 BCE, the epitaph written on his tomb listed his many elected offices, followed by four lines of poetry, bragging about his accomplishments:

By my good conduct, I heaped
honor upon the honor of my family;
I had children, and I tried to equal
the deeds of my father;
I won the praise of my ancestors
and made them glad I was born;
My own virtue has made noble my
family tree.

For generations, the Scipio men had served in high offices. And by the second century BCE, the Scipios had become Rome's leading family. They decorated their family tomb with marble busts of important family members. The oldest sarcophagus contains the body of a Scipio who was a consul of Rome in 298 BCE. Its dedication reads: "Lucius Cornelius Scipio Barbatus, son of Gnaeus, a brave and wise man, whose handsomeness matched his bravery. He was consul, censor, and aedile among you. He captured . . . many cities for Rome and brought home hostages."

“ Statue from Rome, 50–25 BCE

Like other patricians, Scipio Hispanus proudly claimed his ancestors as founding fathers of Rome. He was probably much like the Roman in this statue. Even though scholars cannot tell us this person's name, we can learn a lot just by

As you read

- Keep a list of questions.

- Note **boldfaced** words in text. They are defined in the margins.
  Their *root words* are given in *italics*.

- Look up other unfamiliar words in a dictionary.

- Find important places on the map on pp. 10–11.

- Look up names in Cast of Characters on p. 9 to learn pronunciation.

- Read the sidebars. They contain information to build your understanding.

After you read

- Compare what you have learned with what you thought you would learn before you began the chapter.

looking at him. First: he's a Roman. We know because he's wearing a toga, the garment that was a sign of manhood. The Romans called it the *toga virilis*, and a boy wasn't allowed to wear it until he became a man, usually at 16. Second, because this unknown Roman is carrying masks of his ancestors, we know that his father or grandfather had served as one of Rome's top officials.

These masks, made of wax or clay, usually hung in the hallways of the ancestral home. Romans took them down and carried them in parades and funeral processions.

Roman families were organized like miniature states, with their own religions and governments. The oldest man in the family was called the **paterfamilias**, the patriarch. He was the boss, and his words were law. Scipio Hispanus was the paterfamilias in his family. This meant that he held lifelong power, even over life and death. He could sell or kill a disobedient slave. He had the right to abandon an unwanted baby, leaving him or her outside to die. Usually this would be a sick child or a baby girl to whom the family couldn't afford to give a dowry when she grew up. Romans wanted healthy sons to carry on the family name, yet a father could imprison, whip, disown, or even execute a son who committed a crime. In 63 BCE, a senator named Aulus Fulvius did exactly that after his son took part in a plot to overthrow the government. But this didn't happen very often. Roman fathers were expected to rule their families with justice and mercy, the same way that political leaders were expected to rule the state.

For both the family and the state, religion played a major role in life. Every Roman home had a shrine to the household gods, the Lares. The father served as the family's priest. Scipio Hispanus would have led his family's prayers and made sacrifices to honor their ancestors and please the gods that protected the entire family—living and dead. When a baby was born, Scipio Hispanus would have hit the threshold of his home with an axe and a broom to frighten away any wild spirits that might try to sneak in. When a household member died, Family members carried the body out feet first to make sure that its ghost didn't run back inside. (That's why people still sometimes describe death as "going out feet first.")

vir = "man"
Roman boys donned the *toga virilis* when they became men. *Virilis* is a form of *vir;* "virile" means "manly."

pater + *familias* = "father" + "family"
The paterfamilias was the oldest male member of a Roman family.

TOMBS OF THE SCIPIOS

The Romans believed that the dead should neither be buried nor cremated inside the city walls. They were afraid that Rome's sacred places would become polluted by the presence of death. So they lined the roads leading away from Rome with monuments built to house and honor the dead. Visitors can still see the tombs of the Scipios buried along the Appian Way, about two miles from the Forum. (The Appian Way is a military road that was built in the fourth century BCE.)

The next two pages have models of graphic organizers. You will need these to do the activities for each chapter on the pages after that.

Go back to the book as often as you need to. When you've finished each chapter, check off the standards in the box if you have learned them.

GRAPHIC ORGANIZERS

As you read and study history, geography, and the social sciences, you'll start to collect a lot of information. Using a graphic organizer is one way to make information clearer and easier to understand. You can choose from different types of organizers, depending on the information.

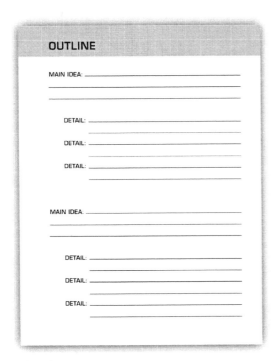

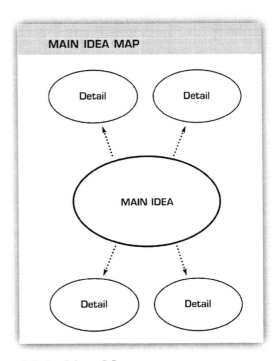

Outline

To build an outline, first identify your main idea. Write this at the top. Then, in the lines below, list the details that support the main idea. Keep adding main ideas and details as you need to.

Main Idea Map

Write down your main idea in the central circle. Write details in the connecting circles.

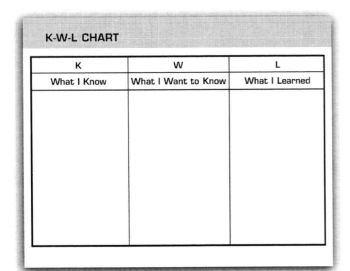

K-W-L Chart

Before you read a chapter, write down what you already know about a subject in the left column. Then write what you want to know in the center column. Then write what you learned in the last column. You can make a two-column version of this. Write what you know in the left and what you learned after reading the chapter.

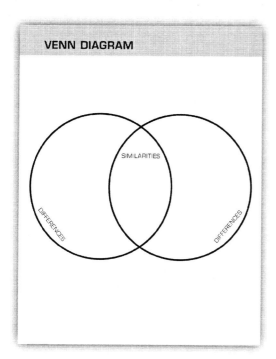

Venn Diagram

These overlapping circles show differences and similarities among topics. Each topic is shown as a circle. Any details the topics have in common go in the areas where those circles overlap. List the differences where the circles do not overlap.

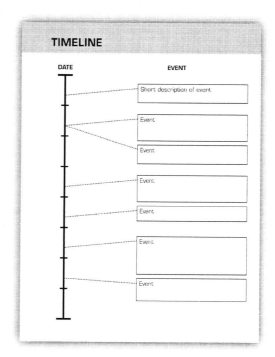

Timeline

A timeline divides a time period into equal chunks of time. Then it shows when events happened during that time. Decide how to divide up the timeline. Then write events in the boxes to the right when they happened. Connect them to the date line.

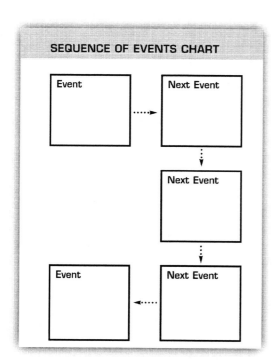

Sequence of Events Chart

Historical events bring about changes. These result in other events and changes. A sequence of events chart uses linked boxes to show how one event leads to another, and then another.

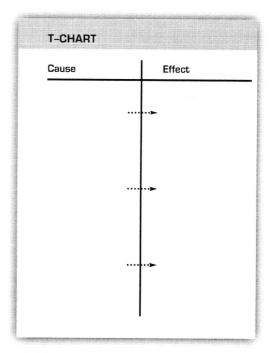

T-Chart

Use this chart to separate information into two columns. To separate causes and effects, list events, or causes, in one column. In the other column, list the change, or effect, each event brought about.

IMPORTANT VOCABULARY WORDS

The Word Bank section of each lesson will give you practice with important vocabulary words from the book. The words below are also important. They're listed in the order in which they appear in each chapter. Use a dictionary to look up any you don't know.

Introduction
miraculous
channel
anonymous
automatically

Chapter 1
migrate
larynx
predator
flourish
carnivore
turmoil
corruption
domesticate

Chapter 2
intermingle
nomadic
livestock
abode
nutrient
cycle
cultivate
inedible
kiln
geometric
ornament
afterlife

Chapter 3
peninsula
proportion
symmetrical

Chapter 4
inscription
sacrifice
slaughter
resolve

Chapter 5
oracle bone
vessel
devour
water table

Chapter 6
merge
isolate
forbidding
domesticate
awesome
mandate
proclamation
resentment
justified
dynastic cycle
out of kilter

Chapter 7
calamity
ingenious
honorary
rite
solemn
inappropriate

Chapter 8
compassionate
ambition
coax
luxury
despise
obedience
treacherous

Chapter 9
lost-wax method
concubine
cocoon
larvae
embroider
pendant
ornament
intricate
diplomatic
banquet
status

Chapter 10
rigid
fundamental
innovation
dutiful
humane
crucial
resolute
honeyed
pious
scornful
ideal
tactic
aggressive
lofty

Chapter 11
scoff
sibling
suburb
ravine

Chapter 12
financial
equivalent
vengeance

Chapter 13
mutilate
favoritism
nontechnical
rarity
poised
consolidate

Chapter 14
hover
manipulate
adept
rebellious
disgruntled
exploit
pretext
prohibition
outmaneuvered
scornful
prominent

Chapter 15
oasis

Chapter 16
potsherd
affectionate

Chapter 17
heavier-than-air
tether
cellulose
fibrous
mechanism

Chapter 18
abundance
empathize
reverence
humiliate
free rein
inferiority
vulgar
dissect
inquiry
flay
vengeful

Chapter 19
prime mover

Chapter 20
nape
mindfulness
crave
Nirvana
obstacle
formidable
reincarnation

Chapter 21
elegant
desolation
domain

Chapter 22
physique
heritage
surpasses

Chapter 23
malaria
charitable
institution
salvation
vegetarianism

Epilogue
dagger-axe
unearthed
scramble

INTRODUCTION: THE CREATION OF THE UNIVERSE

CHAPTER SUMMARY

A Chinese myth tells the story of Pangu, the primordial god from whom the universe sprung. Historians are unsure whether reports of the early Xia Dynasty are based in reality or myth, like the story of Pangu.

ACCESS

All ancient cultures tell stories about their origins. Very often, there are similarities between the stories of different cultures. In your history journal, make a two-column chart. In one column write down details about an origin story that you know. As you read the Introduction, jot down details about the Chinese origin story and compare it with the one you know.

CAST OF CHARACTERS

Write a few words about why the following characters were important.

Pangu (pang goo) _____

Sima Qian (suh-ma cheeyen) _____

Yu (yew) _____

WHAT HAPPENED WHEN?

As you read the chapter, briefly describe the ancient Chinese history sources published in these years.

1040 BCE _____

100 BCE _____

4th century BCE _____

WORD BANK

immortal   dynasty   paleontologist

Complete the sentences with words from the word bank.

1. A _____ is a scientist who studies fossils of extinct animals.

2. A family who rules a country for generation after generation is called a _____.

3. Humans eventually grow old and die, so they are not _____.

WORD PLAY

In the word *immortal*, the starting letters *im-* make up a prefix that means "not." In your history journal, take five minutes and write all the words you can think of that start with *im-*. Ask a parent or partner to do the same. Then read your lists to each other. Use a dictionary to check the meanings of the words on your lists. Put check marks next to the ones in which *im-* means "not."

CRITICAL THINKING
EVALUATING EVIDENCE

The Introduction discusses the story of Yu, supposedly the founder of the Xia dynasty. Modern historians do not think that Yu was a real person, and don't believe that the Xia existed. However, ancient Chinese historians assume that the Xia existed, and they have been right about other things, too.

In the chart, write details from the Introduction about Yu, the Xia dynasty, and what ancient and modern historians say about them. Then write a short paragraph giving your opinion on who is right about the Xia.

Yu	Xia Dynasty	Ancient Historians	Modern Historians

_____

_____

_____

_____

_____

_____

_____

_____

_____

PEKING MAN:
EARLY HUMANS IN CHINA

LEARNING OBJECTIVES

This chapter addresses Content Standards 6.6.1 and 6.6.2. It also addresses the following historical and social sciences analysis skills: Chronological and Spatial Thinking 1, 2, and 3; Research, Evidence, and Point of View 3; Historical Interpretation 1, 2, 3, 4, and 5. A complete list of content standards and analysis skills appears on pages 61–62 of this study guide.

CHAPTER SUMMARY

The remains of approximately forty of China's earliest humans, nicknamed "Peking Man," were discovered in a cave near Beijing (Peking) in 1929. These remains, belonging to the species *Homo erectus*, disappeared during World War II and have not yet been recovered.

ACCESS

Archaeologists and other scientists study fossils and the remains of prehistoric hominids and try to draw conclusions about how they lived. This is the case with the remains of Peking Man, found in Zhoukoudian Cave near Beijing, China. What have these remains told scientists about these hominids? What questions remain unanswered? Copy into your history journal the main idea map graphic organizer from page 8 of this study guide. In the central circle, write *Peking Man*. In the other circles, categorize the details that have been learned, or are still waiting to be learned, about Peking Man.

CAST OF CHARACTERS

In complete sentences, tell what each person has to do with the fossils of Peking Man.

1. Jia Lanpo _____

_____

2. Mao Zedong _____

_____

3. Li Zhaodong _____

_____

WHAT HAPPENED WHEN?

Number these events in the history of *Homo erectus* in the order that they occurred.

_____ *Homo erectus* lives in Java.

_____ *Homo erectus* lives in China.

_____ *Homo erectus* lives in Africa.

WORD BANK

Beijing   hominids   extinct   skullcap   Java

Fill in the blanks with the correct words from the word bank.

1. The remains of the earliest _____ in China were found in a cave near

_____ .

2. The bone at the top of the head is called the _____ .

3. Scientists disagree on whether Peking Man became _____ or lives on in modern Chinese people.

WORD PLAY

The chapter discusses the study of bones that are hundreds of thousands of years old. With a partner, make a list in your history journal of the technical words related to that study that are used in the chapter. Add to your list other such words that you know. Together, define the words. Use a dictionary to find the meanings of the words you don't know.

WORKING WITH PRIMARY SOURCES

Read this ancient Miao folk song, and then answer the questions.

> Heavenly King was intelligent,
> Spat a lot of spittle into his hand,
> Clapped his hands with a noise
> Produced heaven and earth,
> Tall grass made insects,
> Stories made men and demons,
> Made men and demons,
> Made male and made female.
> How is it you do not know?

1. How did Heavenly King create heaven and earth? _____
   _____

2. What might the Miao have connected with the noise that Heavenly King makes by clapping?
   _____

3. What is the difference between the way animals (insects) and humans were created?
   _____

4. Why do you think that the folk song implies that humans and demons were created in the same way?
   _____

ALL OVER THE MAP

Use this map to help you answer the questions.

1. How far away from Beijing is Zhoukoudian Cave? _____

2. What does the small inset map tell you? _____
   _____

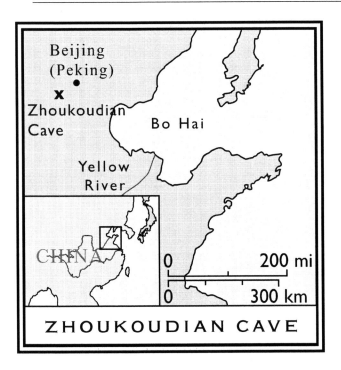

ZHOUKOUDIAN CAVE

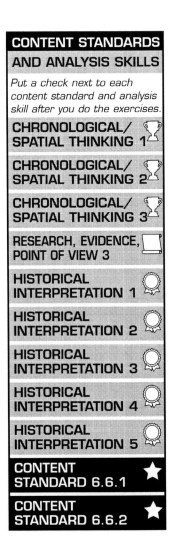

CONTENT STANDARDS AND ANALYSIS SKILLS

Put a check next to each content standard and analysis skill after you do the exercises.

CHRONOLOGICAL/ SPATIAL THINKING 1

CHRONOLOGICAL/ SPATIAL THINKING 2

CHRONOLOGICAL/ SPATIAL THINKING 3

RESEARCH, EVIDENCE, POINT OF VIEW 3

HISTORICAL INTERPRETATION 1

HISTORICAL INTERPRETATION 2

HISTORICAL INTERPRETATION 3

HISTORICAL INTERPRETATION 4

HISTORICAL INTERPRETATION 5

CONTENT STANDARD 6.6.1

CONTENT STANDARD 6.6.2

"SURPRISE AND DELIGHT": THE DISCOVERY OF CHINA'S FIRST CULTURE

CHAPTER SUMMARY

Between 5000 and 3000 BCE, the Yangshao began farming millet along the Yellow River while the Hemudu grew rice in the marshes near Hangzhou Bay. The agricultural revolution meant a more reliable food source, the possibility of permanent settlements, and eventually the development of art, crafts, and writing.

ACCESS

Like other ancient people, the early Chinese were roving hunter-gatherers. Sometime around 7,000 years ago, some began to settle down and became farmers and herders. To highlight the similarities and differences of these two types of lifestyles, make a Venn diagram in your history journal, modeled after the one on page 9 of this study guide. Label one circle *Hunter-Gatherers* and the other circle *Farmer-Herders*; label the area where the circles intersect *Both*. As you read, place details from the chapter in the appropriate areas of the diagram.

CAST OF CHARACTERS

Write brief descriptions of the following characters.

Liu Changshan _____

Johan Gunnar Andersson _____

WORD BANK

artifact   millet   wattle and daub   urns

Connect each word in the word bank with an idea about the first Chinese culture.

1. something that they made _____

2. something that they used to bury people _____

3. something that they built with _____

4. something that they ate _____

CRITICAL THINKING

OUTLINE

Use the outline graphic organizer on page 8 of this study guide to help you organize the information in the chapter about the Yangshao culture. Draw an outline in your history journal. Write the main idea of the outline at the top of the page, and then fill in several details from the chapter beneath each of the following topics.

Topic I: Where they were located

Topic II: How they got food

Topic III: Why they settled along rivers

Topic IV: What their farming practices were

Topic V: What artifacts they made

Topic VI: What their beliefs might have been

ALL OVER THE MAP

Answer the questions about the Yangshao and Hemudu cultures using details from the map.

1. On what bodies of water were the two cultures located?

_____

2. Estimate how far apart the two cultures were. Do you think they had any contact with each other? Why or why not?

_____

_____

_____

_____

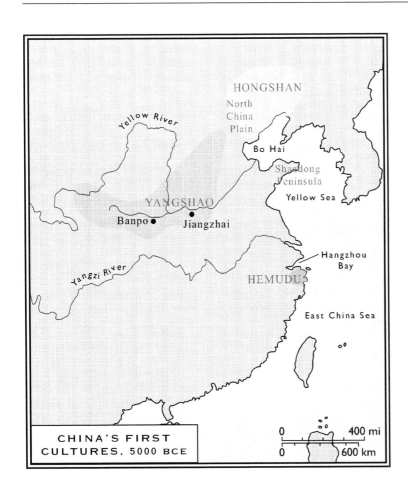

CHINA'S FIRST CULTURES, 5000 BCE

LONGSHAN: CHINA'S FIRST CIVILIZATION

LEARNING OBJECTIVES

This chapter addresses Content Standard 6.6.1. It also addresses the following historical and social sciences analysis skills: Research, Evidence, and Point of View 1, 3, and 4; Historical Interpretation 1, 2, and 6. A complete list of content standards and analysis skills appears on pages 61–62 of this study guide.

CHAPTER SUMMARY

The Longshan civilization, active between 3000 and 2000 BCE, was characterized by stamped-earth defensive walls, weapons, social divisions, and ritual burials. Their crafts included wheel-thrown pottery, jade work, and later bronze and lacquer work.

ACCESS

Look at the diagram of the Longshan tomb on page 32. Note that the pictures of artifacts at the top match the artifacts shown in their places in the grave at the bottom. With a partner, write down questions in your history journal about what you see in the diagram. Speculate what these artifacts can tell archaeologists about the Longshan civilization. Then see how many of your questions are answered by the chapter.

WORD BANK

abrasive   bronze   stamped earth   ritual

Fill in the blanks with the correct words from the word bank.

1. Sand is an _____ substance that can wear away stone.

2. A religious _____ can involve prayers or a feast.

3. The harder metal _____ is made by combining copper and tin.

Write one or two sentences describing the process named by the word that you did not use.

_____

_____

_____

_____

WORD PLAY

The people of the Longshan civilization used jade to make beautiful objects. The word *jade* has multiple meanings. With a partner, list other words from the chapter that have more than one meaning. Use the words in sentences to show their meanings. Write lists and sentences in your history journal.

CRITICAL THINKING
DRAWING CONCLUSIONS

The chapter tells about many artifacts left by the Longshan civilization. However, it is up to archaeologists and other researchers to draw conclusions about what these artifacts mean. Complete the chart by writing what conclusion researchers have drawn from each of the artifacts. Some artifacts can result in more than one conclusion.

Longshan Artifact	Conclusion
A stamped earth wall, 20 feet high and 30 feet wide, was discovered.	
Of 116 stone implements found, 28 were weapons.	
A few graves had many grave goods; most graves had none.	
Beautiful carved jade objects were found in some graves.	
Some jade was worked into the shapes of animals or demons.	
Deer shoulder bones that had cracked after being put in fire were found.	

WORKING WITH PRIMARY SOURCES

Study the pictures of Longshan artifacts on pages 33–35 of your book. Write a paragraph that tells your conclusions about the Longshan craftworkers. Support your conclusions by referring to the artifacts.

_____

_____

_____

_____

_____

_____

_____

_____

CHAPTER 4

EVERYBODY TALKS ABOUT THE WEATHER: AGRICULTURE AND ORACLES

LEARNING OBJECTIVES

This chapter addresses Content Standard 6.6.1. It also addresses the following historical and social sciences analysis skills: Chronological and Spatial Thinking 3; Research, Evidence, and Point of View 3 and 4; Historical Interpretation 1 and 2. A complete list of content standards and analysis skills appears on pages 61–62 of this study guide.

CHAPTER SUMMARY

In 1899, a Chinese scholar named Wang Yirong looked at some "dragon bones" prescribed to him as medicine and realized they were inscribed with ancient Chinese characters. Since that time, scholars have found thousands of oracle bones used by members of the Shang dynasty to communicate with the gods.

ACCESS

Many people today believe that they will have happier, more successful lives if they perform certain rituals. With a partner, make a two-column chart in your history journal. In one column, write examples of modern rituals that you know about. As you read the chapter, write examples of ancient Chinese rituals. When you are finished, compare and contrast the purpose, parts, and hoped-for results of modern and ancient rituals.

WORD BANK

relics   clan   oracle   man-year

Fill in the blanks with the correct words from the word bank.

1. All the members of a _____ claim a common ancestor.

2. A project requires 500 _____ of labor if 100 workers work on it for 5 years.

3. To communicate with the gods, ancient people asked for the help of an _____.

WORD PLAY

The chapter mentions *forecasting* the weather and other events, which means knowing in advance what will happen. The prefix *fore-* can have two meanings: "in advance" and "in front." List all of the words you know that begin with the prefix *fore-*. Use a dictionary if necessary. Group the words according to the meaning of their prefixes.

WITH A PARENT OR PARTNER

Using the Writing Chinese feature on page 42 in your book, work with a partner to create your own symbols for words and ideas. Complete the chart by making up and combining symbols for the words and ideas listed. Then make up symbols for words or ideas you choose.

Word	Symbol	Idea	Symbol
tree		forest	
field		harvest	

ALL OVER THE MAP

Use the map on page 41 to answer these questions.

1. Using the map scale, describe the size of the area ruled by the Shang Dynasty.

_____

2. Why would the area of Shang "influence" be larger than the area the Shang ruled?

_____

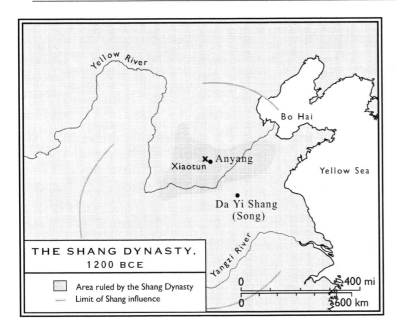

CRITICAL THINKING

Archaeologists have gotten a lot of information about the Shang Dynasty from the oracle bones they have uncovered. Use a main idea map graphic organizer like the one on page 8 of this study guide to organize the knowledge gained this way. Copy the graphic organizer in your history journal. In the central circle, write Information from Oracle Bones. In the surrounding circles, use the headings _How Oracle Bones Were Read_, _What People Asked the Gods_, and _What the Oracle Bones Told People to Do_. Then complete the organizer with details from the chapter.

WORKING WITH PRIMARY SOURCES

Read the oracle bone questions. Then write a paragraph in your history journal explaining the kinds of information the Shang were seeking from their gods.

- "Is it Di [the high god] who is harming our harvest?"
- "Is it the Mountain who is harming the grain?"
- "Is it the Yellow River who is harming the grain?"
- "This season will the locusts reach to this city of Shang?"
- "Should we announce the locusts to the Yellow River?"
- "Should the king go to offer a wine sacrifice and perform the plowing ritual?"
- "When we reach the fourth month, will Di order it to rain?"
- "In praying for harvest, if the sacrifice is performed at sunset, will [the king] receive aid?"

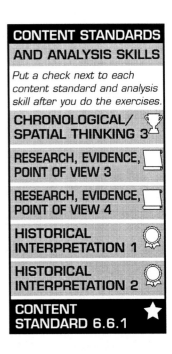

CONTENT STANDARDS
AND ANALYSIS SKILLS

Put a check next to each content standard and analysis skill after you do the exercises.

CHRONOLOGICAL/
SPATIAL THINKING 3

RESEARCH, EVIDENCE,
POINT OF VIEW 3

RESEARCH, EVIDENCE,
POINT OF VIEW 4

HISTORICAL
INTERPRETATION 1

HISTORICAL
INTERPRETATION 2

CONTENT
STANDARD 6.6.1

DRAGON BONES AND HIDDEN TREASURES: THE SHANG COURT

LEARNING OBJECTIVES

This chapter addresses Content Standard 6.6.1. It also addresses the following historical and social sciences analysis skills: Chronological and Spatial Thinking 1 and 2; Research, Evidence, and Point of View 3; Historical Interpretation 1 and 3. A complete list of content standards and analysis skills appears on pages 61–62 of this study guide.

CHAPTER SUMMARY

In 1976, archaeologists uncovered the royal tomb of Lady Hao near Anyang. Discoveries there confirmed the importance of warfare and rigid social distinctions at the Shang court, including the practice of servants following their masters in death. The grave goods also provided many examples of Shang craftsmanship, especially their bronze work.

ACCESS

What can people tell about you from the objects they might find in your room? Archaeologists draw conclusions about ancient civilizations from the artifacts they find in tombs and other sites they excavate. Make a two-column chart in your history journal. As you read the chapter, list artifacts that have been found from the Shang Dynasty in the left column, and draw conclusions about the people who made these things in the right column.

CAST OF CHARACTERS

Write complete sentences describing the significance of each of the following people from the chapter.

Lady Hao _____

_____

Di Xin _____

_____

Sima Qian _____

_____

WHAT HAPPENED WHEN?

1500–400 BCE _____

1500–1046 BCE _____

1976 CE _____

WORD BANK

priceless   tribute   anonymous   piece-mold process

Write the word from the word bank next to its meaning.

1. _____   Gifts sent to royalty to show loyalty

2. _____   Unknown

3. _____   Value that cannot be calculated in money

WORD PLAY

In telling about the people who created the bronze objects of the Shang Dynasty, the authors use two synonyms, or words that mean almost the same thing: *craftsman* and *artisan*. With a partner, use a dictionary or a thesaurus to find other synonyms for these words and explain the how their meanings differ. Write your explanations in your history journals.

CRITICAL THINKING

Reread the description of the piece-mold process the Chinese bronze workers of the 2nd millennium BCE used to make pots and urns. Then in your history journal draw a sequence of events chart (see page 9 of this study guide) to outline the steps in the process. Write the steps in complete sentences, using time order words such as *first, then, next,* and *last*.

WORKING WITH PRIMARY SOURCES

With a partner, read the following poem from the *Book of Poetry (Shijing)*. The poem tells about the activities of common Chinese people around 600 BCE. Using a main idea map like the one on page 8 of this study guide, categorize these activities in two or more ways. For example, one way uses categories such as *farming, other work, religion,* and *duties to the nobles*. See how many ways you can categorize the activities. Draw the main idea map in your history journal and fill it out.

In the fourth month, seeding is the yao grass;
    in the fifth month, singing is the **cicada**.
In the eighth month you should harvest;
    in the tenth month, the trees shed and leaves fall.
In the days of the first month, go and hunt badgers.
Catch those foxes and **raccoon-dogs**
    and make fur garments for a young nobleman. . . .

In the days of the second month,
    cut chunks of ice, dong-dong!
In the days of the third month,
    store them in the ice house.
In the days of the fourth month,
    rise early to present lamb and offer onions.
In the ninth month, things shrivel with the frost;
    in the tenth month, clean the **threshing floor**.
Twin wine vessels are offered as a feast
    and then slaughter lambs and sheep.
Enter that noble hall
    and lift in a toast the **rhino cup**:
May you live forever and without end!

cicada, a winged insect that makes a loud buzzing sound.

raccoon-dog, a type of dog, native to China, that looks very much like a raccoon.

threshing floor, the floor of the room where grain is separated from the harvested plants.

rhino cup, a cup made from a rhino horn

CONTENT STANDARDS AND ANALYSIS SKILLS

Put a check next to each content standard and analysis skill after you do the exercises.

CHRONOLOGICAL/ SPATIAL THINKING 1

CHRONOLOGICAL/ SPATIAL THINKING 2

RESEARCH, EVIDENCE, POINT OF VIEW 3

HISTORICAL INTERPRETATION 1

HISTORICAL INTERPRETATION 3

CONTENT STANDARD 6.6.1

HEAVEN IS BRIGHTLY AWESOME: THE WESTERN ZHOU ERA AND THE MANDATE OF HEAVEN

LEARNING OBJECTIVES

This chapter addresses Content Standard 6.6.1. It also addresses the following historical and social sciences analysis skills: Chronological and Spatial Thinking 1, 2, and 3; Research, Evidence, and Point of View 1, 2, 4, and 5; Historical Interpretation 1, 2, and 3. A complete list of content standards and analysis skills appears on pages 61–62 of this study guide.

CHAPTER SUMMARY

The Western Zhou Era (1045–771 BCE) marked the beginning of the enduring Chinese idea of the Mandate of Heaven, the belief that heaven chose a virtuous man to rule and would support a ruling family only as long as they performed their responsibilities faithfully.

ACCESS

This chapter introduces the Mandate of Heaven, or the Chinese belief that a ruling dynasty could gain or lose the support of the gods depending on their actions. Before reading the chapter, create a K-W-L chart in your history journal like the one on page 8 of this study guide. In the first column, write what you know about Chinese rulers. In the second column, write questions about the Mandate of Heaven that you want to have answered. As you read the chapter, write the answers to the questions.

CAST OF CHARACTERS

Write a brief description of each of the following people related to the Zhou dynasty.

Jiang Yuan _____

Wen _____

Wu _____

Cheng _____

Duke of Zhou _____

You _____

WHAT HAPPENED WHEN?

In your history journal, make a copy of the timeline graphic organizer on page 9 of this study guide, and divide the line into hundred-year sections, starting at 1100 BCE and ending at 700 BCE. Arrange the important personalities of the Zhou Dynasty along the timeline. (Check their dates in the Cast of Characters on pages 9–11 of *The Ancient Chinese World*.) Include important events during that time, including natural events that seemed to show that the Mandate of Heaven was shifting.

WORD BANK

heaven   barbarians   impassable   virtuous   legitimate

Fill in the blanks with the correct words from the Word Bank.

When the Zhou rulers came to power, many of their subjects thought they were

_____, or uncivilized foreigners. This was because China was surrounded by nearly

_____ barriers, and so contact with outsiders was limited. However, when the Zhou

king Cheng won several battles, it looked as if _____ were on his side. This helped

establish the Zhou as the _____, or rightful, rulers of China.

WORD PLAY

The adjective *virtuous* is made by adding the suffix *-ous* to the noun *virtue*. Use a dictionary to find the meaning of the noun and the suffix, and then combine the meanings to arrive at the meaning of *virtuous*. Write five more *-ous* words on the lines, and explain their meanings.

_____

_____

_____

_____

_____

ALL OVER THE MAP

Use the map on page 52 of the book and the description of China's geography on page 53 to show the physical features that isolated China from the world. Draw in the mountains and indicate the desert areas. Then label these features on the map.

Manchuria   Taklamakan Desert   Yellow Sea

Mongolia   Kunlun Mountains   East China Sea

Gobi Desert   Himalayas   South China Sea

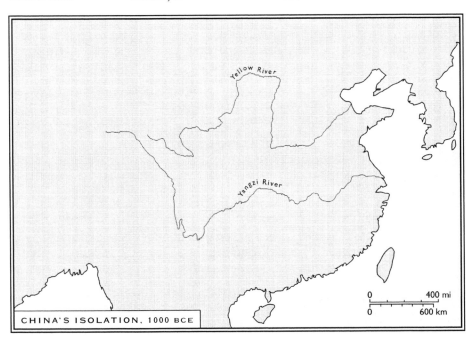

CHINA'S ISOLATION, 1000 BCE

WRITE ABOUT IT

Write a three-paragraph essay in your history journal telling your opinion about whether a shift in the Mandate of Heaven could actually be seen in the events of the time or if it was recognized only by Chinese historians looking back at the deposed rulers. Use details from the chapter to support your opinion.

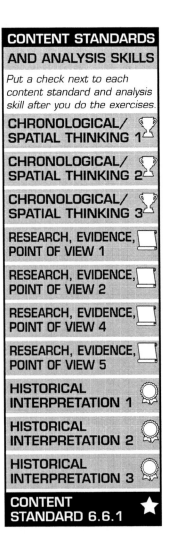

CONTENT STANDARDS AND ANALYSIS SKILLS

Put a check next to each content standard and analysis skill after you do the exercises.

CHRONOLOGICAL/ SPATIAL THINKING 1

CHRONOLOGICAL/ SPATIAL THINKING 2

CHRONOLOGICAL/ SPATIAL THINKING 3

RESEARCH, EVIDENCE, POINT OF VIEW 1

RESEARCH, EVIDENCE, POINT OF VIEW 2

RESEARCH, EVIDENCE, POINT OF VIEW 4

RESEARCH, EVIDENCE, POINT OF VIEW 5

HISTORICAL INTERPRETATION 1

HISTORICAL INTERPRETATION 2

HISTORICAL INTERPRETATION 3

CONTENT STANDARD 6.6.1

WHO'S IN CHARGE?
THE RISE OF THE HEGEMONS

LEARNING OBJECTIVES

This chapter addresses Content Standards 6.6.3 and 6.6.4. It also addresses the following historical and social sciences analysis skills: Chronological and Spatial Thinking 1; Research, Evidence, and Point of View 1 and 2; Historical Interpretation 1, 3, and 5. A complete list of content standards and analysis skills appears on pages 61–62 of this study guide.

CHAPTER SUMMARY

Unpopular Zhou leaders weakened the Zhou's grip on China. They became so weak that the people turned to a powerful nobleman named Duke Huan of Qi to protect them. Duke Huan became the first of five hegemons, nobles who took over the political and military functions of weak kings.

ACCESS

The period discussed in this chapter was one of confusion in China. To help keep track of the events, draw a timeline in your history journal modeled on the graphic organizer on page 9 of this study guide. Write the events of this time in order on the timeline, and add dates to the events where you can.

CAST OF CHARACTERS

Briefly describe the following people from the chapter.

King Li _____

King You _____

Bao Si _____

Duke Huan of Qi _____

Jiu _____

Gao Xi _____

Quan Zhong _____

WHAT HAPPENED WHEN?

Describe the rulers of China in these periods:

9th century BCE _____

after 771 BCE _____

685–643 BCE _____

WORD BANK

hierarchy   hegemon   philosopher   allegiance

Complete the sentences with words from the word bank.

In ancient China, the powerful lords owed _____ to the king. However, if the king

were weak, the lords might choose a _____ to take control of the country in

dangerous times. The king would still be at the top of the _____, but the affairs of

the country would be run by the most powerful lord.

CRITICAL THINKING
FACT OR OPINION

The Zhou and the Hegemon

A fact is a statement that can be proven. An opinion is a statement that cannot be proved or disproved. Read the chapter, and for each statement about the Zhou kings and the hegemons below, write an *F* or an *O* to indicate whether it is a fact or an opinion.

_____ The Chinese king sometimes had a difficult time controlling the lords.

_____ The lords had their own armies.

_____ King Li was the worst of the Zhou kings .

_____ The Chinese lords' greatest fear was being invaded by barbarians.

_____ After the Zhou capital was destroyed, the Chinese lords looked to Duke Huan of Qi to set things right.

_____ Duke Huan had the best government in the Zhou Dynasty.

_____ Huan was aided in governing by his assistant Guan Zhong.

_____ Guan Zhong, who had been Huan's enemy, should not have gone to work for Huan.

CAUSE AND EFFECT

Read the chapter, and create in your history journal a cause and effect graphic organizer similar to the T-chart on page 9 of this workbook. Below is a list of causes and effects from the chapter that relate to the rule of the hegemon Duke Huan of Qi. Match the causes with their effects in the columns of your graphic organizer.

CAUSE	EFFECT
The Eastern Zhou kings were weak military leaders,	SO Huan made Guan Zhong his most important minister.
Guan Zhong supported a duke who lost a conflict with Duke Huan,	SO the other lords chose Huan as the first hegemon when invasion threatened.
Guan Zhong was a talented government official,	SO other states began to attack Zhou territory.
Together, Huan and Guan Zhong ran Qi's government very efficiently,	SO Guan Zhong should have committed suicide.

WRITE ABOUT IT

Imagine that you are a Chinese historian living about 200 years after the reign of Duke Huan. What would your opinion be about the role that Guan Zhong played in the history of Qi? Write an essay in your history journal either criticizing or supporting Guan Zhong. Support your opinion with details from the chapter.

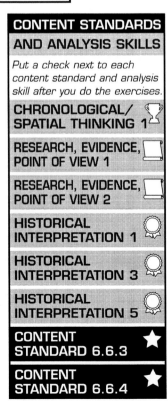

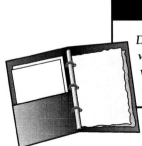

HISTORY JOURNAL

Don't forget to share your history journal with your classmates, and ask if you can see what their journals look like. You might be surprised—and get some new ideas.

THE STORY OF SHENSHENG: SACRIFICE AND STATEHOOD

LEARNING OBJECTIVES

This chapter addresses Content Standard 6.6.4. It also addresses the following historical and social sciences analysis skills: Chronological and Spatial Thinking 1; Research, Evidence, and Point of View 1, 3, and 5; Historical Interpretation 1. A complete list of content standards and analysis skills appears on pages 61–62 of this study guide.

CHAPTER SUMMARY

The story of Shensheng illustrates the ancient Chinese values of obedience, sacrifice, and honor, and focuses on traditional practices of Chinese religion.

ACCESS

Who are you loyal to? Which people do you honor? How do you show your respect for other people? Who did ancient Chinese people honor, and how did they do it? Before reading the chapter, create in your history journal a K-W-L chart like the one on page 8 of this study guide. In the first column, write down notes about the people you honor in your daily life and how you honor them. Maybe you honor your parents or family members by listening to what they say or giving them presents. In the second column, write questions about how the ancient Chinese might have honored people. As you read the chapter, write answers to your questions in the third column.

CAST OF CHARACTERS

On the lines, briefly describe the relationships between these people from the chapter.

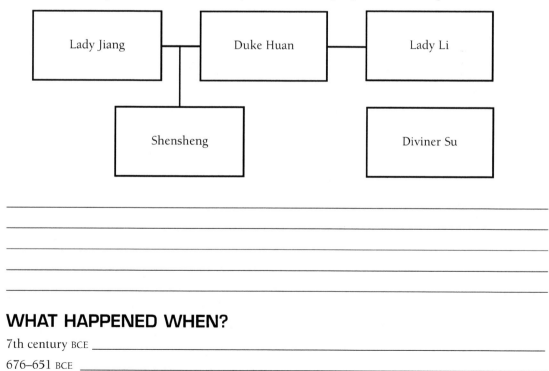

Lady Jiang — Duke Huan — Lady Li

Shensheng

Diviner Su

_____

_____

_____

_____

_____

WHAT HAPPENED WHEN?

7th century BCE _____

676–651 BCE _____

4th century BCE _____

WORD BANK

diviner   reverse psychology   sacred   personator

Fill in the blanks with the correct words from the word bank.

1. A _____ is a person who reads signs from nature to foretell the future.

2. Someone who would take the place of a dead ancestor in a religious ceremony is known as a

   _____.

3. Artifacts that are needed for a religious ceremony would be considered to be _____.

WORD PLAY

On the lines, write an example of the term that you did not use in the sentences above.

_____

_____

_____

CRITICAL THINKING
CATEGORIZING

In your history journal, create a T-chart like the one at the back of this study guide. Reread the story of Shensheng. Find the events in the story involving ancient Chinese worship practices or beliefs. Describe each one in the left column of the chart. In the right column, tell which of the following aspects of Chinese belief each one represents.

- Reading signs to foretell the future
- Sacrifice
- Power of dreams
- Ritual
- Being loyal to one's lord
- Obeying one's ancestors

WITH A PARENT OR PARTNER

What might have happened if Lady Li had been brought to trial for her actions in the story of Shensheng? Was she a bad person, worthy of the fate she ultimately received? Or was she just trying to use the system to gain power for herself and her son? In your history journals, have one partner write down what she might have said in her own defense, while the other partner writes down what the brothers of Shensheng would have said about her. Discuss your comments about Lady Li using the perspective of 7th century BCE China.

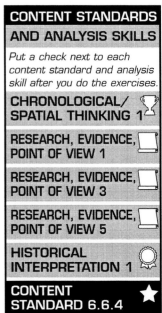

GROUP TOGETHER

Wouldn't it be interesting to talk to other students about ancient Chinese values? How are they like or different from values today? Get a few friends together and ask your teacher to help you organize a discussion group at school. Have one person take notes and another person present the group's ideas to the class.

CONTENT STANDARDS AND ANALYSIS SKILLS

Put a check next to each content standard and analysis skill after you do the exercises.

CHRONOLOGICAL/ SPATIAL THINKING 1

RESEARCH, EVIDENCE, POINT OF VIEW 1

RESEARCH, EVIDENCE, POINT OF VIEW 3

RESEARCH, EVIDENCE, POINT OF VIEW 5

HISTORICAL INTERPRETATION 1

CONTENT STANDARD 6.6.4

FROM BRONZE TO PLASTIC: CRAFTS IN EVERYDAY LIFE

LEARNING OBJECTIVES

This chapter addresses Content Standard 6.6.4. It also addresses the following historical and social sciences analysis skills: Chronological and Spatial Thinking 1; Research, Evidence, and Point of View 3; Historical Interpretation 2 and 6. A complete list of content standards and analysis skills appears on pages 61–62 of this study guide.

CHAPTER SUMMARY

Scholars know very little about the lives of ordinary people in ancient China because so little written and physical evidence of their lives remain. But historians can deduce some information from luxury objects like the lacquer boxes, jade dagger, and bronze vessels found in the tomb of the Marquis of Zeng.

ACCESS

What artifacts did the ancient Chinese cultures leave behind? What do we know about their crafts and workmanship? To explore these questions, in your history journal create a main idea map graphic organizer similar to the one on page 8 of this study guide. In the center circle, write *Ancient Chinese Crafts*. Then, as you read the chapter, write the names of the crafts that we know the Chinese were skilled in. Include details about each craft in the circle.

CAST OF CHARACTERS

Explain why historians know so much about the Marquis of Zeng's life.

_____

_____

WHAT HAPPENED WHEN?

Using a timeline in your history journal (see graphic organizer on page 9 of this study guide), arrange the following events from the chapter chronologically from top to bottom on the timeline. Include dates (actual or approximate) for each event. Then answer the questions.

> Marquis Yi of Zeng buried
> Chinese producing enough silk to trade
> Chinese begin carving jade

1. Which event occurred during the Neolithic Age? _____

2. How many years ago was the Marquis of Zeng buried? _____

3. Which occurred first, jade carving or silk trading? _____

WORD BANK

disintegrate/durable   marquis/maidservant   lacquer/resin

On the lines, describe how the words in each pair above are related to each other.

1. _____

   _____

2. _____

   _____

3. _____

   _____

WORD PLAY

The chapter says that the Chinese prized jade, which is a *semiprecious* stone. The word *semiprecious* is made up of the prefix *semi-* and the base word *precious*. Use a dictionary to find the definitions of both parts, and write them in your history journal. Then find and define five more words that begin with *semi-*, and write sentences using those words.

CRITICAL THINKING

OUTLINE

Three processes are described in detail in the chapter: the lost-wax method of bronze-working, making clothing from silk, and using lacquer to make objects. In your history journal, create an outline like the one on page 8 of this guide. Use the outline to organize the details of each process.

Topic I: The Lost-Wax Method of Making Bronze Objects

Topic II: Making Clothing from Silk

Topic III: Making Useful Objects Out of Lacquer

COMPREHENSION

SUMMARIZING

The chapter describes the work of a number of people who served the Marquis of Zeng and other wealthy and powerful people in 5th century BCE China. On the lines, identify the craftspeople and workers discussed in the chapter. Then summarize what each one of these workers did.

_____

_____

_____

_____

_____

_____

WRITE ABOUT IT

Imagine you are Shuwan, the maidservant of one of the wives of the Marquis of Zeng. Write a journal entry in your history journal describing a day in your life. Use a conversational tone, as if you are telling a friend about your life. Include your opinions about the people you serve, and describe the objects that you handle for your mistress.

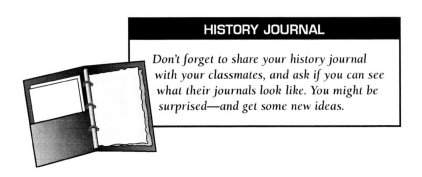

HISTORY JOURNAL

Don't forget to share your history journal with your classmates, and ask if you can see what their journals look like. You might be surprised—and get some new ideas.

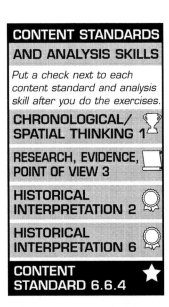

CONTENT STANDARDS AND ANALYSIS SKILLS

Put a check next to each content standard and analysis skill after you do the exercises.

CHRONOLOGICAL/ SPATIAL THINKING 1

RESEARCH, EVIDENCE, POINT OF VIEW 3

HISTORICAL INTERPRETATION 2

HISTORICAL INTERPRETATION 6

CONTENT STANDARD 6.6.4

A WISE MAN AND HIS FOLLOWERS: CONFUCIUS AND CONFUCIANISM

LEARNING OBJECTIVES

This chapter addresses Content Standards 6.6.3 and 6.6.4. It also addresses the following historical and social sciences analysis skills: Chronological and Spatial Thinking 1; Research, Evidence, and Point of View 3, 4, and 5; Historical Interpretation 1 and 2. A complete list of content standards and analysis skills appears on pages 61–62 of this study guide.

CHAPTER SUMMARY

Confucius was born during a time of political instability during the 6th century BCE. He developed a philosophy of order, obedience, and benevolence that continues to influence China.

ACCESS

WITH A PARENT OR PARTNER

Share with a parent or partner important ideas that you have heard or read about humans, how we live our lives, and how we relate to other people. If you can, identify the source of the idea. Discuss the importance of such ideas for a large, complex society.

CAST OF CHARACTERS

Using information from the chapter as well as the Cast of Characters list on pages 9–11 of *The Ancient Chinese World,* write three or four facts about each of these Chinese thinkers.

Confucius (con-FYU-shus) _____

_____

_____

_____

Mencius (men-shus) _____

_____

_____

_____

Mozi (mwoh-dzuh) _____

_____

_____

_____

WHAT HAPPENED WHEN?

On the lines, number the events of Confucius' life in chronological order.

_____ Becomes a teacher

_____ Has sayings collected in *Analects*

_____ Starts a school

_____ Becomes a government official

WORD BANK

Kongfuzi   proverbs   righteousness   calligraphy   *junzi*

Fill in the blanks with the correct words from the Word Bank.

1. The Chinese philosopher _____ is well known for his short

   _____, or sayings about life.

2. He was a great thinker who was interested in how _____ and justice can be
   achieved on earth.

3. One of the things he taught in his school was _____, which was an art as well as
   a form of communication.

WORD PLAY

In the chapter, find the word that you did not use in the sentences above. In your own words,
describe the sort of person this word names.

_____

_____

CRITICAL THINKING
IDENTIFYING POINT OF VIEW

The chapter says that Confucius felt that changes were dangerous for society and ruined people's
character, and that people needed to return to the way they had behaved in earlier generations.
Explain how Confucius set forth this traditional way of thinking for his students in the following
areas.

1. Education _____

_____

2. Society _____

_____

3. Family _____

_____

THINK ABOUT IT

The chapter says this about the philosopher Mozi, who lived after Confucius:

> In the Confucian ideal, it's natural to love members of one's own family more than
> strangers and people from your own country more than foreigners. Mozi rejected
> this, saying that loving some people more than others led to behavior that was
> against the Will of Heaven, such as stealing, heavy taxation, and injustice of all kinds.

In your history journal, write an essay agreeing or disagreeing with Mozi's point of
view. Include ideas and details from the chapter to support your opinion.

WORKING WITH PRIMARY SOURCES
EVALUATING POINT OF VIEW

Read the following excerpt from *The Analects* of Confucius. In your history journal,
write a paragraph about this excerpt telling

- what you think applies to the modern world, and why.
- what you think does not apply to the modern world, and why.

> Wealth and a good reputation are what everybody wants, but if you cannot get
> them by sticking to your own Way, you should not keep them. Poverty and low
> status are what everyone despises but if I get them by following my Way, I will not
> avoid them. If a gentleman avoids humaneness, how can he make a worthy name
> for himself? The gentleman does not abandon humaneness for an instant, even if
> he is in a hurry or in difficulties.

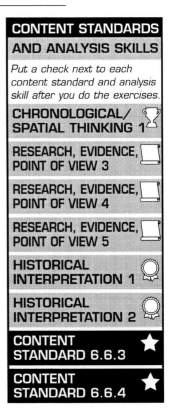

CONTENT STANDARDS AND ANALYSIS SKILLS

Put a check next to each content standard and analysis skill after you do the exercises.

CHRONOLOGICAL/ SPATIAL THINKING 1

RESEARCH, EVIDENCE, POINT OF VIEW 3

RESEARCH, EVIDENCE, POINT OF VIEW 4

RESEARCH, EVIDENCE, POINT OF VIEW 5

HISTORICAL INTERPRETATION 1

HISTORICAL INTERPRETATION 2

CONTENT STANDARD 6.6.3

CONTENT STANDARD 6.6.4

THE WAY: LAOZI

LEARNING OBJECTIVES

This chapter addresses Content Standard 6.6.3. It also addresses the following historical and social sciences analysis skills: Chronological and Spatial Thinking 1 and 2; Research, Evidence, and Point of View 3 and 4; Historical Interpretation 1 and 2. A complete list of content standards and analysis skills appears on pages 61–62 of this study guide.

CHAPTER SUMMARY

Laozi was the possibly legendary writer of the *Daodejing*, or *Classic Text of the Way and Virtue*. This book of mostly short, catchy phrases, lays out the principles of the Way, which is supposed to be the pattern of the universe. When the world has the Way, life is good and orderly; when it lacks the Way, life is chaotic and dangerous.

ACCESS

The chapter discusses the *Daodejing*, which may or may not have been written by a man named Laozi, who supposedly lived about the time of Confucius. The *Daodejing* criticized the teachings of Confucius and the other Chinese philosophers discussed in the preceding chapter. Read this chapter with a partner to find instances of differences between the *Daodejing* and the teachings of Confucius. In your history journal, make a T-chart like the one on page 9 of this study guide to contrast the two philosophies.

CAST OF CHARACTERS

On the lines, describe the kind of person Laozi was supposed to have been. Include details about his appearance and his way of speaking.

_____

_____

_____

WHAT HAPPENED WHEN?

In your history journal, use information in the chapter about the following dates to write a paragraph explaining why historians think that the version of the *Daodejing* we know today is close to the original version.

    500 CE   168 BCE   300 BCE

WORD BANK

Daodejing archivist frugality tranquility

Fill in the blanks in the sentences with the words above.

According to legend, the author of the _____ was an _____ who

lived in China about the time of Confucius. Some of the sayings in this book talk about the value of

_____, or not spending wastefully. Others talk about how _____

and weakness can overcome action and strength.

WORD PLAY

The words in the Word Bank are all made up of word parts. They are either compound words or words-plus-suffixes. Use information from the chapter or from a dictionary to separate each word into its parts and write a definition.

1. Daodejing _____

2. archivist _____

3. frugality _____

4. tranquility _____

WORKING WITH PRIMARY SOURCES
DRAWING CONCLUSIONS

With a partner, read these statements from the *Daodejing*. Then work together to answer the questions in your history journal. Use complete sentences.

> The world is a sacred vessel and cannot be controlled. If you try to control it, you will ruin it; if you try to seize it, you will lose it.
>
> Sincere words are not beautiful and beautiful words are not sincere.
>
> The Way is great; Heaven is great; Earth is great; and the king is also great. In the country there are four greats, and the king occupies one place among them.

1. What does the first statement seem to be saying about how humans should interact with the natural world?

2. Is the second statement saying that you can't give another person a compliment? Explain your answer.

3. Why might the third statement be troubling for a Chinese king during this time in history?

IN YOUR OWN WORDS

In your history journal, paraphrase these statements as if you were telling them to a friend in everyday speech.

WRITE ABOUT IT

The *Daodejing* gives advice that can be used to govern a country. In your history journal, write a sheet of instructions in your own words for a ruler based on the statements from the *Daodejing* in the chapter. Be sure to include terms such as *the Way, nonaction, yin, yang, balance,* and *peace.*

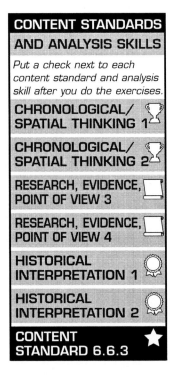

CONTENT STANDARDS AND ANALYSIS SKILLS

Put a check next to each content standard and analysis skill after you do the exercises.

CHRONOLOGICAL/ SPATIAL THINKING 1

CHRONOLOGICAL/ SPATIAL THINKING 2

RESEARCH, EVIDENCE, POINT OF VIEW 3

RESEARCH, EVIDENCE, POINT OF VIEW 4

HISTORICAL INTERPRETATION 1

HISTORICAL INTERPRETATION 2

CONTENT STANDARD 6.6.3

HISTORY JOURNAL

Don't forget to share your history journal with your classmates, and ask if you can see what their journals look like. You might be surprised—and get some new ideas.

12

THE ART OF WAR: WARFARE IN ANCIENT CHINA

LEARNING OBJECTIVES

This chapter addresses Content Standards 6.6.1 and 6.6.2. It also addresses the following historical and social sciences analysis skills: Chronological and Spatial Thinking 1; Research, Evidence, and Point of View 1, 3, and 5, Historical Interpretation 1, 2, 3, and 5. A complete list of content standards and analysis skills appears on pages 61–62 of this study guide.

CHAPTER SUMMARY

During the Spring and Autumn Period, a career military man named Sun Wu wrote a book that has since become a classic: *The Art of War.* The publication of this work marked a sea change in Chinese military history, which was in the midst of a transition from limited warfare to ferocious, large-scale battles.

ACCESS

Read the first page of the chapter, and then answer the following questions in complete sentences in your history journal.

1. The first paragraph talks about how the ancient Chinese handled conflicts. What similarities do you see between ancient China and the present world?

2. The second paragraph talks about the effects of war on soldiers in ancient China. Compare and contrast this with what you know about the effects on modern American soldiers of having to go to war.

CAST OF CHARACTERS

Briefly describe the significance of each of the following characters.

Sun Wu (swun woo) _____

Mao Zedong _____

WHAT HAPPENED WHEN?

Match the dates to their significance for the history of war in China.

_____ 1. 1600–1450 BCE   a. *The Art of War* written by Sun Wu

_____ 2. 5th century BCE   b. Battle deaths reach 100,000

_____ 3. 341 BCE   c. Battle deaths reach 450,000

_____ 4. 260 BCE   d. Chariot comes into use in China

WORD BANK

incentive   strategist   guerrilla   deception   submission

Answer the questions using the words in the Word Bank.

1. What name would you use for a person who plans military operations?

_____

2. What word names a reason that makes people want to do something?

_____

3. What word would you use to describe making an opponent believe you are stronger than you are?

_____

4. What word would you use to describe an army that has surrendered?

_____

WORD PLAY

Write a definition of the word in the Word Bank that you didn't use to answer the questions above. Then write a *homonym* for that word, or a word that sounds the same but has a different spelling and meaning. Then use both of the words in a single sentence.

_____

_____

_____

CRITICAL THINKING
CAUSE AND EFFECT

Read the chapter, and in your history journal, create a cause and effect graphic organizer similar to the T-chart on page 9 of this study guide. Below is a list of causes and effects from the chapter that relate to the changes in warfare in ancient China. Match the causes with their effects in the columns of your graphic organizer.

CAUSE	EFFECT
War was a financial strain on families who provided soldiers,	SO kings began choosing commanders based on their abilities rather than their birth.
Chariots were difficult to use in mountainous, lake-filled South China,	SO inventors and strategists had to come up with better weapons and ways to fight.
As conflicts increased, military forces became larger and more important,	SO soldiers began to wear metal armor .
The crossbow was powerful enough to kill a soldier through his leather armor,	SO swords were developed for use in fighting at close range.

WORKING WITH PRIMARY SOURCES
IN YOUR OWN WORDS

In your history journal, rewrite these thoughts from *The Art of War*. Use complete sentences.

1. Warfare is the Way of Deception. If you are capable of accomplishing something, seem incapable; if you are close, seem distant; if you are distant, seem close.

2. He will win who knows when to fight and when not to fight.

3. To fight and conquer in all your battles is not supreme excellence; supreme excellence consists in breaking the enemy's resistance without fighting.

WITH A PARENT OR PARTNER

The chapter gives a number of examples of advice that Sun Wu had on how to wage war successfully. With your partner, reread these statements from *The Art of War*. Then discuss how a general or a king could carry out these directives. For example, how can a general know an enemy? What would the general have to understand to "know yourself." In your discussion, try to come to a conclusion about which of the directives would be most important in 5th century BCE China.

CONTENT STANDARDS AND ANALYSIS SKILLS

Put a check next to each content standard and analysis skill after you do the exercises.

CHRONOLOGICAL/ SPATIAL THINKING 1 🏆

RESEARCH, EVIDENCE, POINT OF VIEW 1

RESEARCH, EVIDENCE, POINT OF VIEW 3

RESEARCH, EVIDENCE, POINT OF VIEW 5

HISTORICAL INTERPRETATION 1

HISTORICAL INTERPRETATION 2

HISTORICAL INTERPRETATION 3

HISTORICAL INTERPRETATION 5

CONTENT STANDARD 6.6.1 ⭐

CONTENT STANDARD 6.6.2 ⭐

CHINA GOES IMPERIAL: THE RISE OF THE UNIFIED STATE

LEARNING OBJECTIVES

This chapter addresses Content Standard 6.6.5. It also addresses the following historical and social sciences analysis skills: Chronological and Spatial Thinking 1, 2, and 3; Research, Evidence, and Point of View 1, 3, and 5; Historical Interpretation 1, 2, and 3. A complete list of content standards and analysis skills appears on pages 61–62 of this study guide.

CHAPTER SUMMARY

The disorder of the Eastern Zhou was followed by the brilliant, brutal reign of Shi Huangdi, the First Emperor. The First Emperor promulgated a series of reforms that helped unify his country, including standardizing the written language, weights and measures, the legal system, and even cart-widths.

ACCESS

This chapter is about the first Chinese empire. What does the word *empire* mean to you? With a partner, brainstorm questions about an empire: who rules it, how it is governed, how big it is, what differences there might be across it, and so on. As you read the chapter, see how many of your questions it answers.

CAST OF CHARACTERS

Write a short description of each person.

Shang Yang (shahng yahng) _____

Ying Zheng (ing jehng) _____

Prince Dan _____

Jing Ke (jing kuh) _____

What does the name *Shi Huangdi* mean? Which one of the people above used this name?

_____

WHAT HAPPENED WHEN?

1. When did Shang Yang help Qin become a strong state? _____

2. When did Ying Zheng create the first Chinese empire? _____

3. When did Shi Huangdi die? _____

4. When was Shi Huangdi's mausoleum discovered? _____

WORD BANK

Jin mausoleum terracotta consequence seared

Fill in the blanks with the correct words from the Word Bank.

1. Ancient Chinese would say that something which weighed about a pound was a _____.

2. Many _____ statues were found in the _____ of the dead emperor.

3. The memory of the crash was _____ into my brain.

WORD PLAY

The writer Sima Qian used this sentence in telling the story of the attempted assassination of Ying Zheng: "Day and night I have gnashed my teeth and seared my heart for such a plan." *Gnashed my teeth* and *seared my heart* are examples of sensory images that help the reader understand the general's feelings. On the lines, write more sensory images that show strong emotion, either love or hate.

_____

_____

CRITICAL THINKING
SEQUENCE OF EVENTS

Read the chapter, and in your history journal create a sequence of events graphic organizer similar to the one on page 9 of this study guide Place the following events in the life of Shi Huangdi in order in the graphic organizer.

- Begins to conquer neighboring states
- Becomes "First Emperor"
- Becomes ruler of Qin
- Failed assassination attempt by Jing Ke
- Unifies most of China
- Institutes reforms in China
- Puts down revolt against his rule
- Dies and is buried in mausoleum

DRAWING CONCLUSIONS

Using details from the chapter, answer these questions in complete sentences.

1. Do you think people were more likely to respect Shi Huangdi or fear him? Why?

_____

_____

2. Was the job of unifying China completed when Shi Huangdi conquered the neighboring states? Or was there more work to do? Explain your answer.

_____

_____

WRITE ABOUT IT

Pick one of the three reforms that Shi Huangdi introduced to his empire (see page 97 of the book): standardization of Chinese writing; direct rule from central government; or standard weights, measures, and cartwidths. In your history journal, write an essay discussing what you see as the positive or negative effects of the reform. Write from the perspective of one of Shi Huangdi's subjects.

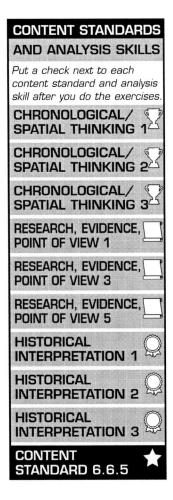

CONTENT STANDARDS
AND ANALYSIS SKILLS

Put a check next to each content standard and analysis skill after you do the exercises.

CHRONOLOGICAL/ SPATIAL THINKING 1

CHRONOLOGICAL/ SPATIAL THINKING 2

CHRONOLOGICAL/ SPATIAL THINKING 3

RESEARCH, EVIDENCE, POINT OF VIEW 1

RESEARCH, EVIDENCE, POINT OF VIEW 3

RESEARCH, EVIDENCE, POINT OF VIEW 5

HISTORICAL INTERPRETATION 1

HISTORICAL INTERPRETATION 2

HISTORICAL INTERPRETATION 3

CONTENT STANDARD 6.6.5

KINGS AND COMMONERS: LIU BANG AND THE FOUNDING OF THE HAN DYNASTY

LEARNING OBJECTIVES

This chapter addresses Content Standard 6.6.6. It also addresses the following historical and social sciences analysis skills: Chronological and Spatial Thinking 1 and 2; Research, Evidence, and Point of View 1, 3, and 4; Historical Interpretation 1, 2, and 3. A complete list of content standards and analysis skills appears on pages 61–62 of this study guide.

CHAPTER SUMMARY

When the First Emperor died while traveling, one of his courtiers disguised the death and forged a message to the heir to the throne telling him that his father wished him to commit suicide. Huhai, another of the First Emperor's sons, ruled briefly before being defeated by a coalition of dissatisfied aristocrats, led by Xiang Yu, and peasants, led by the former bandit Liu Bang. Liu Bang won the civil war that followed and established the Han dynasty, one of China's greatest.

ACCESS

Shi Huangdi was the First Emperor of China, but many states resisted his rule and the rule of his sons. Why was the change from one ruler to another the cause for violence and war in ancient China? Was it because of the people who became emperor? Was it because of the way an empire is run, with all power held by one person? Or was it some combination of factors? Keep these questions in mind as you read the chapter.

CAST OF CHARACTERS

Write a short description of each character.

Liu Bang (leeoh bahng) _____

Fusu _____

Huhai (hoo-hi) _____

Zhao Gao (jaow gaow) _____

Xiang Yu (sheeahng yew) _____

Chen She (chen shuh) _____

Xiang Zhuang (sheeahng jwahng) _____

WHAT HAPPENED WHEN?

Copy the timeline graphic organizer on page 9 of this study guide into your history journal, and arrange the events from the chapter chronologically from top to bottom on the timeline.

Chen She is killed.

Liu Bang occupies imperial capital.

Liu Bang becomes leader of Pei province.

Liu and Xiang battle for control of the empire.

Xiang Yu takes capital from Liu Bang.

Huhai becomes emperor.

Liu Bang becomes leader of bandits.

Liu Bang becomes emperor; beginning of Han Dynasty.

Xiang Yu and Chen She rebel against Huhai.

Shi Huangdi dies.

WORD BANK

ting bureaucracy peasant aristocrat *Gaozu*

Fill in the blanks with the correct words from the Word Bank.

1. A ruler needs a _____ to run the government.

2. An _____ comes from a higher social class than a _____.

In your own words, define the Chinese terms.

3. *ting* _____

4. *Gaozu* _____

WORD PLAY

A *bureaucrat* is someone who works in a *bureaucracy*. An *aristocrat* is someone who is a member of an *aristocracy*. With a partner, think of another pair of words that ends in *-crat* and *-cracy*. Then use a dictionary to find the meaning of *-crat* and *-cracy*. Use the definitions to make up your own words with those endings.

_____

_____

CRITICAL THINKING
COMPARE AND CONTRAST

In your history journal, draw a Venn diagram like the one on page 9 of this study guide. Use it to compare and contrast Liu Bang and Xiang Yu. Include details from the chapter about each man from these categories:

• Background

• Supporters

• Military Successes

• Treatment of Others

WORKING WITH PRIMARY SOURCES
ANALYZING A PRIMARY SOURCE

Read the speech that Liu Bang gave after Xiang Yu challenged him to a duel in 204 BCE. Then answer the questions.

> You as a vassal killed your lord, you killed those who had already surrendered, you governed unjustly, and you led people in taking an oath then did not keep to it. The world has no place for a traitor without principles. I am leading my righteous troops, in obedience to the various lords, to execute the remaining bandits. I would send a criminal who managed to escape execution to strike you down. Why should I bother to fight a duel with you myself?

1. In your own words, restate the accusation that Liu Bang makes against Xiang Yu.

_____

2. Why does Liu Bang call Xiang Yu a "traitor without principles"?

_____

3. How does Liu Bang make his cause sound like the better one?

_____

4. Why would the last two sentences of the speech be so insulting to Xiang You?

_____

_____

CONTENT STANDARDS AND ANALYSIS SKILLS

Put a check next to each content standard and analysis skill after you do the exercises.

CHRONOLOGICAL/ SPATIAL THINKING 1

CHRONOLOGICAL/ SPATIAL THINKING 2

RESEARCH, EVIDENCE, POINT OF VIEW 1

RESEARCH, EVIDENCE, POINT OF VIEW 3

RESEARCH, EVIDENCE, POINT OF VIEW 4

HISTORICAL INTERPRETATION 1

HISTORICAL INTERPRETATION 2

HISTORICAL INTERPRETATION 3

CONTENT STANDARD 6.6.6

WHO IS CHINESE?
ETHNIC GROUPS AND CHINA

LEARNING OBJECTIVES

This chapter addresses Content Standards 6.6.2, 6.6.5, and 6.6.6. It also addresses the following historical and social sciences analysis skills: Chronological and Spatial Thinking 1 and 3; Research, Evidence, and Point of View 1 and 3; Historical Interpretation 1, 2, and 3. A complete list of content standards and analysis skills appears on pages 61–62 of this study guide.

CHAPTER SUMMARY

Expansion under the Qin and Han brought the ethnic Chinese people into more frequent contact with outsiders, whom they called by a variety of names, all having the connotation of "barbarians." Royal Han women were sometimes married to "barbarians" with whom the Chinese hoped to negotiate alliances. The construction of the Great Wall of China was an attempt to reduce the risk of invasion by nomad peoples.

ACCESS

Read the title of the chapter. Can you tell "who is Chinese"? Or who is Spanish, or American, or Vietnamese, or Mexican? How do people identify themselves with one ethnic group or another? In a group of three or four of your classmates, read the sidenote defining *ethnic group* on page 107. Discuss what ethnic groups are represented in your small group, in your class, and in your school. What makes each group distinctive? What links the groups together? In your history journal, draw a diagram showing how different groups are interconnected.

CAST OF CHARACTERS

Briefly describe each character.

Wang Zhaojun _____

Yang Liwei _____

WHAT HAPPENED WHEN?

Answer these questions about the construction of the Great Wall of China.

1. When did the Chinese start building walls to keep out wandering tribes? _____

2. Who first turned these barriers into a "great wall"? When did this occur?

   _____

3. Under which dynasty did the Great Wall cross the Gobi Desert? When did this occur?

   _____

WORD BANK

ethnic group   seminomadic   lingered   irritated   intimidating

Use the words in the word bank to complete the sentences.

1. The longer that the barbarians _____ on the edges of the empire, the more
   _____ the Chinese rulers became.

2. The people of an _____ share many characteristics.

3. The attacking forces were turned back by the _____ appearance of the armed fortress.

WORD PLAY

The prefix *semi-* in *seminomadic* means "half" or "partially." With one or two partners, think of other words that have prefixes that tell about size or quantity in the same way; for example, *semicircle* ("half circle") or *quadrilateral* ("four sides"). Try to list words that represent as many different "numbers" as you can.

CRITICAL THINKING
DRAWING CONCLUSIONS

The Chinese felt contempt for their neighbors, whom they called "barbarians." However, they still had to deal with these people. By answering these questions, draw conclusions about the relationship between the Chinese and other ethnic groups.

1. What does the fact that huge numbers of people were absorbed into Chinese culture show about Chinese attitudes toward others?

   _____

   _____

2. What does the construction of the Great Wall of China show about the respect that the Chinese had for the military threat of their neighbors?

   _____

   _____

3. What did the Chinese hope to achieve by giving women from the imperial family as brides to the rulers of nomadic tribes?

   _____

   _____

WRITE ABOUT IT

Imagine that you are Wang Zhaojun looking back on your life as the wife of a Xiongnu ruler. In your history journal, write a letter to one of your sisters telling what makes you happy about your life, and what causes you regret.

ALL OVER THE MAP

The Han rulers pushed the borders of China beyond what they had been before. On the map, show how far the borders extended as you answer the questions.

1. The Han controlled the area of Korea, a large peninsula that sticks out southward from the mainland into the Yellow Sea. Find Korea and label it. Color it in red pencil.
2. The Han also pushed westward to the Taklamakan Desert. Label that desert, and color that area yellow.
3. Northward, the Han conquered territory that had been held by the Xiongnu people. Label the area of the Xiongnu on the map.
4. The Han extended the Great Wall across the Gobi Desert. Measure the parts of the wall that existed under the Han. Using the mileage scale, estimate the length of the Great Wall at that time. Write your answer here.

_____

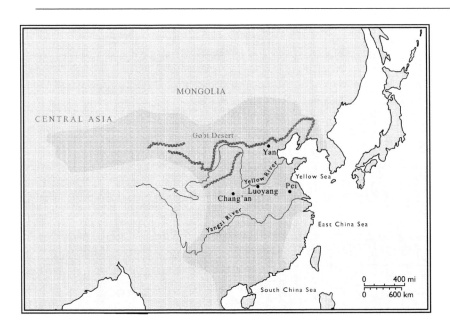

HARD WORK AND HUMILITY: WOMEN IN ANCIENT CHINA

LEARNING OBJECTIVES

This chapter addresses Content Standard 6.6.6. It also addresses the following historical and social sciences analysis skills: Chronological and Spatial Thinking 2; Research, Evidence, and Point of View 1, 2, 3, 4, and 5; Historical Interpretation 1, 4, and 5. A complete list of content standards and analysis skills appears on pages 61–62 of this study guide.

CHAPTER SUMMARY

Chinese women lived restricted lives based on service to their families. Women were taught that their lives should be shaped by humility, hard work, and religious observance.

ACCESS

What roles did women have in ancient China? Did all women have the same kind of life, or did their lives differ depending on whether they were rich or poor, lived in a city or the country, or were educated or uneducated? With a partner, make up a list of interesting questions about women's lives in ancient China. Write them in your history journal. As you read the chapter, check off the questions that are answered. Figure out why others of your questions went unanswered.

CAST OF CHARACTERS

Write a short description of each person.

Ban Zhao (bahn jaow) _____

Feng Yan _____

WHAT HAPPENED WHEN?

1. What period in Chinese history did Ban Zhao write about in the excerpt that begins the chapter?

   _____

2. How many years had passed between the end of that period and the time that Ban Zhao wrote *Precepts for Women*?

   _____

WORD BANK

humility   shaman   magistrate

Fill in the blanks with the correct words from the Word Bank.

1. A person shows _____ by bowing before the king.

2. To communicate with the spirit world, the ancient Chinese might seek the help of a

   _____.

3. Two arguing people would bring their case before a _____ to decide who is right.

WORD PLAY

The chapter says that *cinnabar* is a reddish mineral used as a dye. Think of other words that are synonyms for *red*. Use resources such as a dictionary, thesaurus, or a box of crayons or colored pencils. Make a list in your history journal and write down how these words differ from *red*.

CRITICAL THINKING

OUTLINING

What was life like for women in ancient China? Use the outline graphic organizer on page 8 of this study guide to organize the information in your history journal. Take your main ideas from the quote from Ban Zhao that begins the chapter. Write the title of the outline at the top of the page, and then fill in several details from the chapter beneath each of the following topics.

Topic I: Women were lowly and weak.

Topic II: Women should work hard.

Topic III: Women's main duty was performing the sacrifices in her home.

COMPARING AND CONTRASTING

To compare and contrast the works of Ban Zhao and Fen Yang, copy the following chart in your history journal. Then complete the chart.

Question	Ban Zhao	Feng Yan
1. What is the author's purpose for writing this work?		
2. What kind of language does the author use?		
3. What impression do you get about women in ancient China from this document?		
4. What impression do you get about men in ancient China from this document?		

WRITE ABOUT IT

Put yourself in the place of Feng Yan's wife. What would you say to the magistrate about your husband? How would you defend your actions? In your history journal, write a letter to the court showing her side of the story. Use language that shows your personality, as Feng Yan did in his letter.

GROUP TOGETHER

Wouldn't it be interesting to talk to other students about the role of women in ancient China? How are are women's lives different today? Get a few friends together and ask your teacher to help you organize a discussion group at school. Have one person take notes and another person present the group's ideas to the class.

CHAPTER 17

NEW WAYS OF DOING THINGS: INVENTIONS AND TECHNOLOGY

LEARNING OBJECTIVES

This chapter addresses Content Standard 6.6.6. It also addresses the following historical and social sciences analysis skills: Chronological and Spatial Thinking 1 and 2; Research, Evidence, and Point of View 1 and 3; Historical Interpretation 1, 2, 3, and 6. A complete list of content standards and analysis skills appears on pages 61–62 of this study guide.

CHAPTER SUMMARY

The ancient Chinese excelled at technological innovation. Among the many contributions of ancient China were wheelbarrows, kites, rudders, fore-and-aft rigging, compasses, gunpowder, and, above all, paper.

ACCESS

Have these questions in mind as you read this chapter:

- What things did the ancient Chinese invent?
- In what form do I know these inventions?
- What needs did the Chinese have to fill with these inventions?
- How did other people use these inventions?

When you have finished reading the chapter, answer these questions. You can write your answers in your history journal, or discuss the questions in a small group.

WHAT HAPPENED WHEN?

Make a copy of the timeline graphic organizer (see page 9 of this study guide) in your history journal. Place the following inventions in chronological order on the timeline, with their approximate dates.

- wheelbarrow
- fore-and-aft rigging
- paper
- gunpowder
- boat's rudder

WORD BANK

terrain   incentive   firearms   rudder   navigation

On the blank before each sentence, write in the word from the word bank that is a synonym for the word in bold type.

_____ 1. The wheelbarrow was made for carrying heavy things over rough **ground**.

_____ 2. Early boats had no **mechanism for steering**.

_____ 3. Gunpowder was originally used for fireworks, but was later used in **guns**.

_____ 4. There is usually some **important reason** for people to invent new things.

WITH A PARENT OR PARTNER

The chapter discusses advances the ancient Chinese made in *navigation*, including the rudder, fore-and-aft rigging, and the compass. What other navigation-related words do you know? With a parent or partner, see which of you can list the most navigation words in two minutes. When time is up, go over your lists together and tell what each word means. Use a dictionary or another reference source, if necessary.

CRITICAL THINKING
CAUSE AND EFFECT

In your history journal create a cause and effect graphic organizer similar to the one on page 9. Listed below are causes and effects from the chapter that relate to inventions made by the ancient Chinese. Match the causes with their effects in the columns of your graphic organizer.

CAUSE	EFFECT
The huge Chinese armies were constantly in need of food and equipment,	SO inventors had an incentive to come up with improvements in navigation.
Far-flung soldiers needed to communicate with each other,	SO wheelbarrows were invented to carry heavy supplies over rocky, mountainous terrain.
Travel on China's many rivers was an inexpensive and rapid way to trade goods,	SO inventors made compasses that accurately showed directions.
Sailing ships had to wait for winds that were blowing in the direction they were going,	SO kites with multiple colors and shapes may have been invented to send coded messages.
Knowing exactly where thunder came from or birds flew to was important in divining the meaning of omens,	SO inventors came up with fore-and-aft rigging so boats could travel where they wanted to go despite the wind direction.

MAKING INFERENCES

Use the following details to make inferences about the effects that some of the inventions mentioned in the chapter had on the economy of ancient China. How would these inventions help traders and customers? Write your inferences in complete sentences.

1. A single person can use a wheelbarrow to move heavy things over land that is too rocky or mountainous for larger wheeled vehicles.

_____

_____

2. Things made out of paper can be "whiter than fox fur and softer than cotton."

_____

_____

3. Boats with fore-and-aft rigging can travel in a certain direction even if the wind is blowing against them.

_____

_____

READ MORE

To read more about Chinese inventions, see the Further Reading suggestions at the end of *The Ancient Chinese World.*

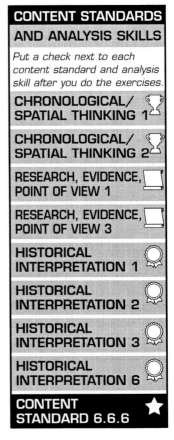

CONTENT STANDARDS
AND ANALYSIS SKILLS

Put a check next to each content standard and analysis skill after you do the exercises.

CHRONOLOGICAL/
SPATIAL THINKING 1

CHRONOLOGICAL/
SPATIAL THINKING 2

RESEARCH, EVIDENCE,
POINT OF VIEW 1

RESEARCH, EVIDENCE,
POINT OF VIEW 3

HISTORICAL
INTERPRETATION 1

HISTORICAL
INTERPRETATION 2

HISTORICAL
INTERPRETATION 3

HISTORICAL
INTERPRETATION 6

CONTENT
STANDARD 6.6.6

POWER AND PERSONALITY: WANG MANG

LEARNING OBJECTIVES

This chapter addresses Content Standard 6.6.6. It also addresses the following historical and social sciences analysis skills: Chronological and Spatial Thinking 1 and 2; Research, Evidence and Point of View 3; Historical Interpretation 1, 2, and 4. A complete list of content standards and analysis skills appears on pages 61–62 of this study guide.

CHAPTER SUMMARY

In 9 CE, an intelligent and ambitious government official named Wang Mang managed to get himself named emperor of the Xin Dynasty. Although he was an effective reformer, his dynasty lasted only fifteen years before a combination of flood, famine, and rebellion toppled his government and led to a restoration of the Han dynasty.

ACCESS

As you read the chapter, answer the following questions in complete sentences in your history journal.

1. How did power change hands in the Chinese empire?

2. Why did power change hands this way?

CAST OF CHARACTERS

Describe the significance of the following characters.

Wang Mang (wahng mahng) _____

Empress Dowager _____

WHAT HAPPENED WHEN?

45 BCE _____

9 CE _____

25 CE _____

WORD BANK

Classics of Rites   dowager   Xin

Fill in the blanks with the correct words from the Word Bank.

1. A _____ is the widow of an important man.

2. _____ tells about Chinese ritual during the Zhou dynasty.

3. The Chinese word for "new" is _____.

CRITICAL THINKING
CAUSE AND EFFECT

The life of Wang Mang was filled with ups and downs. Something would happen, and his career would be on the upswing. Then something else would happen and his influence would decrease. For each of the following causes, fill in the effect on Wang Mang's career.

CAUSE	EFFECT
1. Wang's father dies.	
2. Wang's Uncle Feng commends Wang to the empress dowager and emperor.	
3. Emperor Cheng dies, and Wang's grandmother loses power at court.	
4. The new emperor dies, and Wang's grandmother regains her power at court.	
5. Wang becomes prime minister and puts a nine-year-old boy on the throne.	
6. The young emperor dies and Wang puts a two-year-old emperor on the throne.	
7. Wang becomes emperor and makes many reforms in the old way of doing things.	
8. Rebellious groups attack the capital city.	

DRAWING CONCLUSIONS

Answer these questions to draw conclusions about Chinese society in the time of Wang Mang.

1. What was the best way for a young man to get ahead in the Chinese court of that time?

_____

_____

2. Why was being sent away from the imperial court a major blow to Wang Mang's career?

_____

_____

3. What inequalities existed in Chinese society at that time?

_____

_____

4. What ultimately cost Wang Mang his throne?

_____

_____

A NEW RELATIONSHIP WITH THE GODS: THE RISE OF DAOISM

LEARNING OBJECTIVES

This chapter addresses Content Standard 6.6.3. It also addresses the following historical and social sciences analysis skills: Chronological and Spatial Thinking 1; Research, Evidence, and Point of View 1 and 3; Historical Interpretation 1 and 2. A complete list of content standards and analysis skills appears on pages 61–62 of this study guide.

CHAPTER SUMMARY

In 142 CE, a man named Zhang Ling said that Laozi, author of the *Daodejing*, appeared to him and told him about a new kind of religion in which "The gods do not eat or drink." This religion, which emphasized the moral character of the gods, is today called Daoism.

ACCESS

Read the opening sentence of the chapter. What would you do if a god appeared to you and told you to start a new religion? What would you have to do to fulfill this mission? How would it change your life? Write down your thoughts on starting a new religion in your history journal, and then compare them to the events in the life of Zhang Ling.

CAST OF CHARACTERS

Write a descriptive sentence about each of the following characters from the chapter.

Zhang Ling (jahng ling) _____

_____

Zhang Lu (jahng loo) _____

_____

Laozi (laow-dzuh) _____

_____

WHAT HAPPENED WHEN?

142 CE _____

180–215 CE _____

WORD BANK

divinity   *qi*   **repentant**

Fill in the blanks with the correct words from the word bank.

1. A god is immortal, and so has _____.

2. According to the Chinese, a person's energy or vitality is his or her _____.

3. Someone who is _____ wants to make up for bad deeds in the past.

CRITICAL THINKING

Use the following chart to explain the major ideas of the religion started by Zhang Ling. In the right column, write details about each idea listed in the left column.

1. New relationship with gods: "The gods do not eat or drink."	
2. The Dao is the major ruling principle of the universe.	
3. The highest deities are the Three Celestial Worthies.	
4. The next highest-ranking deities are the Officers of Heaven, Earth, and Water.	
5. The followers of the Dao would be among the "seed people."	
6. Daoism was more than just a religion; it was a way of life.	

WRITE ABOUT IT

For the China during the Han dynasty, the Daoist religion and state presented some revolutionary ideas, from their ideas about the gods to their ideas about people and the way they should relate to each other. In your history journal, write an essay comparing the Daoist society with the larger society of the Han dynasty.

GROUP TOGETHER

Wouldn't it be interesting to talk with other students about the main ideas of Daoism? How is it similar to or different from other religions you know about? Get a few friends together and ask your teacher to help you organize a discussion group at school. Have one person take notes and another person present the group's ideas to the class.

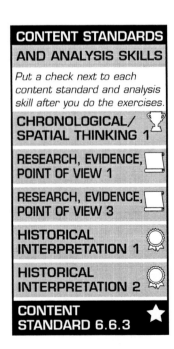

CONTENT STANDARDS
AND ANALYSIS SKILLS

Put a check next to each content standard and analysis skill after you do the exercises.

CHRONOLOGICAL/ SPATIAL THINKING 1 🏆

RESEARCH, EVIDENCE, POINT OF VIEW 1 ▢

RESEARCH, EVIDENCE, POINT OF VIEW 3 ▢

HISTORICAL INTERPRETATION 1 🏅

HISTORICAL INTERPRETATION 2 🏅

CONTENT STANDARD 6.6.3 ★

"A GOLDEN MAN": BUDDHISM AND THE SILK ROAD

LEARNING OBJECTIVES

This chapter addresses Content Standards 6.6.2, 6.6.7, and 6.6.8. It also addresses the following historical and social sciences analysis skills: Chronological and Spatial Thinking 1, 2, and 3; Research, Evidence, and Point of View 1 and 3; Historical Interpretation 1, 2, 3, and 6. A complete list of content standards and analysis skills appears on pages 61–62 of this study guide.

CHAPTER SUMMARY

The religion of Buddhism was carried to China along the Silk Road by Buddhist traders from other countries. Once in China, the religion had to be adapted to be accepted by the people.

ACCESS

Buddhism came to China from India. But how would a religion that developed in one area relate to the people from a totally different area? Use the K-W-L chart on page 8 of this study guide to help you learn more. In the "What I Know" column, write what you already know about how new ideas come to a people from elsewhere and what happens to those ideas in their new home. Fill in the "What I Want to Know" column with your questions, and as you read the chapter, write the answers to your questions and other interesting facts in the "What I Learned" column.

CAST OF CHARACTERS

Write a descriptive sentence about each of the following characters from the chapter.

Siddhartha Gautama (si-DARTH GOW-tam) _____

_____

Emperor Ming _____

_____

Xiang Kai _____

_____

WHAT HAPPENED WHEN?

Use information from the chapter to answer the following questions.

1. About what years did the Buddha live? How can you tell?

_____

2. When did Buddhism become known in China? How can you tell?

_____

3. Was there a close relationship between the silk trade and the appearance of Buddhism in China? How can you tell?

_____

WORD BANK

xiang jiao   karma   enlightened one   craving   intercepted

Fill in the blanks with the correct words from the word bank.

1. The worship of images, or _____ is very important in Chinese Buddhism.
2. The ancient Sanskrit word *Buddha* means _____.
3. In Buddhism, the overall sum of the good and bad deeds in your life is your_____.
4. One of the aims of Buddhism is to get people to stop _____ material riches.

WORD PLAY

The word *intercepted* has two parts: the prefix *inter-* ("between") and *-cepted* ("take").

1. Find *intercepted* near the bottom of page 136. Use the definitions of the word parts above to explain the word's use in this context.

_____

_____

2. Use a dictionary to find two more examples of words that begin with *inter-*. Write sentences using those words correctly.

_____

_____

CRITICAL THINKING

ANALYZING DIFFERENCES

Use the following chart to analyze the differences in South Asian and Chinese Buddhism. For each practice or concept in South Asian Buddhism, write why it was difficult for the Chinese to understand.

South Asian Buddhist Concept or Practice	Why It Was Difficult for Chinese to Understand
1. Buddhist monks leave their families and never marry.	
2. Buddhist monks shave their heads.	
3. Eternity is imagined in millions of years.	
4. The soul is eternal, and is reborn into another body after death.	
5. There is no point to making sacrifices. The Buddha is not a god.	

UNDERSTANDING THE MAIN IDEA

In your history journal, answer these questions in complete sentences.

1. What caused the Silk Road to become a flourishing trade route between China and Rome?
2. What effects did Buddhism have on the Chinese?

ALL OVER THE MAP

Use the map of the Silk Road on page 135 to answer these questions in your history journal.

1. Approximately how long is the section of the Silk Road shown on the map?
2. What physical obstacles faced traders along the route?

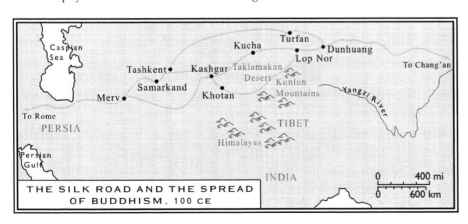

THE SILK ROAD AND THE SPREAD OF BUDDHISM, 100 CE

"SOMEONE WITH THE TALENT TO COMMAND": A GENERAL TAKES CHARGE

LEARNING OBJECTIVES

This chapter addresses Content Standard 6.6.6. It also addresses the following historical and social sciences analysis skills: Chronological and Spatial Thinking 1; Research, Evidence, and Point of View 1, 3, 4, and 5; Historical Interpretation 1, 2, 5, and 6. A complete list of content standards and analysis skills appears on pages 61–62 of this study guide.

CHAPTER SUMMARY

By the beginning of the 3rd century CE, the Han dynasty was threatened by both court intrigues and the emergence of rebel groups like the Yellow Turbans. A remarkable poet/general named Cao Cao rose through the ranks of the army and instituted a series of reforms before his death.

ACCESS

How did the government of the late Han dynasty work? To answer this question, in your history journal create a main idea map similar to the one on page 8 of this study guide. In the central circle, write *Late Han Government*. As you read the chapter, fill in the surrounding circles with details about the prime minister Cao Cao, the reforms he made, and the battles he fought.

CAST OF CHARACTERS

Write a descriptive sentence about each of these characters.

Cao Cao (tsaow tsaow) _____

Yellow Turbans _____

Liu Bei (leeoh bay) _____

WHAT HAPPENED WHEN?

Briefly describe what happened on the following dates.

189 CE _____

196 CE _____

220 CE _____

WORD BANK

devastation   advantageous   opulent   annexing

On the blank before each sentence, write in the word from the word bank that is a synonym for the word in bold type.

_____ 1. The battlefield was a picture of **destruction** after the armies left.

_____ 2. The Chinese empire grew in size by **adding** neighboring lands to its territory.

_____ 3. The Chinese imperial court lived in **extravagant** surroundings.

CRITICAL THINKING
MAIN IDEA AND DETAILS

In your history journal, create a main idea map graphic organizer like the one on page 8 of this study guide. In the central circle, write "Influence of Cao Cao." Then, in the surrounding circles, write details from the chapter that tell how the rule of Cao Cao benefited the Chinese of the Han dynasty. Label the surrounding circles "Peace," "Economy," "Fairness," and "Government."

WORKING WITH PRIMARY SOURCES

Read this commentary on Cao Cao, which appears in *The World in Ancient Times Primary Sources and Reference Volume*. Then, in your history journal, explain what the commentary says about Cao Cao's character.

> When young, Cao Cao was fond of falconry and racing dogs. He was dissolute and unrestrained. His uncle would often mention this to Song [his father], and Cao was worried about this. Later he ran into his uncle on the road. He put on a fallen face and a crooked mouth and when his uncle, thinking this strange, asked the reason, he said, "I have caught some evil disease." The uncle informed Song of this. Song was frightened and summoned Cao Cao, but his face and mouth were the same as always. Song asked, "Your uncle said you caught a disease, are you better already?" Cao replied, "I never caught a disease, I have just lost the love of my uncle, so he sees what is not there." Song's doubts were raised, and from that time, whatever the uncle told him about Cao Cao, he didn't believe him.

EVALUATING POINT OF VIEW

The end of the chapter notes that later sources had different opinions of Cao Cao. Many admired his intelligence, talents, and boldness, but others said he was a villain with magic powers. In your history journal, write an essay that evaluates each point of view: Why would people believe this about Cao Cao?

HISTORY JOURNAL

Don't forget to share your history journal with your classmates, and ask if you can see what their journals look like. You might be surprised—and get some new ideas.

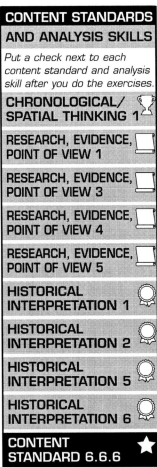

CONTENT STANDARDS
AND ANALYSIS SKILLS

Put a check next to each content standard and analysis skill after you do the exercises.

CHRONOLOGICAL/
SPATIAL THINKING 1

RESEARCH, EVIDENCE,
POINT OF VIEW 1

RESEARCH, EVIDENCE,
POINT OF VIEW 3

RESEARCH, EVIDENCE,
POINT OF VIEW 4

RESEARCH, EVIDENCE,
POINT OF VIEW 5

HISTORICAL
INTERPRETATION 1

HISTORICAL
INTERPRETATION 2

HISTORICAL
INTERPRETATION 5

HISTORICAL
INTERPRETATION 6

CONTENT
STANDARD 6.6.6

22

A "BARBARIAN" LEADER: THE THREE KINGDOMS AND LIU YUAN

LEARNING OBJECTIVES

This chapter addresses Content Standard 6.6.8. It also addresses the following historical and social sciences analysis skills: Chronological and Spatial Thinking 1, 2, and 3; Research, Evidence, and Point of View 3 and 4; Historical Interpretation 1. A complete list of content standards and analysis skills appears on pages 61–62 of this study guide.

CHAPTER SUMMARY

After his father Cao Cao's death, Cao Pi declared himself emperor of the Wei dynasty. A Han relative, Liu Bei, declared himself emperor of the Han state. A third warlord, Sun Quan, declared himself ruler of the Wu state. The resulting period of unrest and confusion is called the Three Kingdoms era.

ACCESS

The period of the Three Kingdoms was a turbulent, confusing time. To follow the events of the era, make a three-column chart in your history journal. Label the columns *Wei*, *Han*, and *Yu*. As you read the chapter, jot down notes about the rival states in your chart.

CAST OF CHARACTERS

Write a sentence describing each of the following characters.

Cao Pi (tsaow pee) _____

Liu Bei (leeoh bay) _____

Sun Quan (swun chooen) _____

Simas (suh-mas) _____

Liu Yuan (leeoh yewen) _____

WHAT HAPPENED WHEN?

Create a timeline graphic organizer like the one on page 9 of this study guide in your history journal. Place the following dates on the timeline with a short description of what happened for each one.

184 CE	196 CE	215 CE	220 CE	221 CE	222 CE
263 CE	265 CE	280 CE	304 CE	310 CE	

WORD BANK

yuan   enterprise

Complete each sentence with a word from the word bank.

1. A person's _____ is his or her business or work.

2. In China, a deep, almost bottomless pit might be called _____.

CRITICAL THINKING

Use the outline graphic organizer on page 8 of this study guide to help you organize the information about the rise and fall of the Three Kingdoms. Write the main idea of the outline at the top of the page in your history journal, and then fill in several details from the chapter beneath each of the following topics.

Topic I: Wei

Topic II: Han

Topic III: Wu

Topic IV: Jin

ALL OVER THE MAP

Use the map on page 144 of *The Ancient Chinese World* to answer these questions. Use complete sentences.

1. Name the Three Kingdoms in order from north to south.

_____

2. Which state was the largest? Which was the smallest?

_____

3. Distance was a problem for the rulers of Wei when they tried to conquer Wu. How far away are the two states?

_____

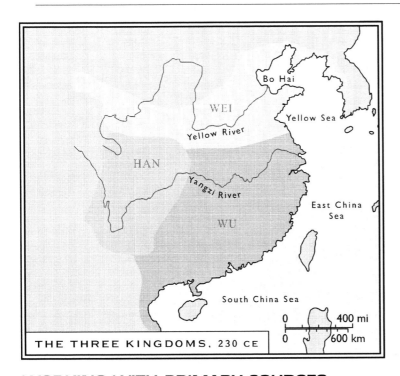

THE THREE KINGDOMS, 230 CE

WORKING WITH PRIMARY SOURCES

Although China during this period was racked by military conflict, stories show that the people still believed in maintaining their values. Read the following excerpt, which appears in *The World in Ancient Times Primary Sources and Reference Volume*. Then, in your history journal, write a moral for the tale.

Xun Jubo came a long way to look after a friend who was ill. Just then the barbarians were attacking the county seat and his friend said to Jubo, "I am about to die. You should go!" Jubo said, "I came from afar to see that you are alright. You order me to go, but forsaking my honor to save my own life, how could that be something this Xun Jubo would do?" When the bandits arrived, they said to Jubo, "When the great army arrived the entire county was empty. What kind of man are you, that you dare to stay here alone?" Jubo replied, "My friend is sick and I couldn't bear to leave him. I would like to offer my own life in place of my friend's." The bandits all said to each other, "We are a bunch of fellows lacking in honor and we have entered an honorable country." Then they marshaled their troops and returned home and the entire county escaped harm.

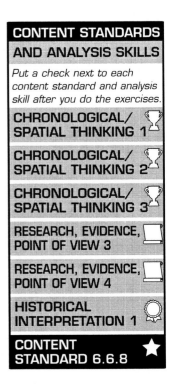

CHAPTER

23

A FOREIGN GOD UNITES CHINA: BUDDHISM AFTER THE HAN

LEARNING OBJECTIVES

This chapter addresses Content Standard 6.6.8. It also addresses the following historical and social sciences analysis skills: Chronological and Spatial Thinking 1; Research, Evidence, and Point of View 1 and 3; Historical Interpretation 1, 2, and 3. A complete list of content standards and analysis skills appears on pages 61–62 of this study guide.

CHAPTER SUMMARY

The fall of the Han in 220 CE ushered in 350 years of political disorder so severe that a significant proportion of the population emigrated to the south, away from barbarian invasions and violence. Over the next few centuries, the Chinese people increasingly turned to Buddhism as a way to make sense of their difficult lives.

ACCESS

After the fall of the Han dynasty, China experienced centuries of chaos. Governments rose and fell, trade dwindled, life was dangerous and unpredictable. What do people do when faced with such conditions? What do they hold on to while events are swirling around them. With a partner, make predictions about how the Chinese people coped with the chaos of this period based on your knowledge of Chinese history and beliefs. Write the predictions down in your history journal. As you read, check your predictions for accuracy.

CAST OF CHARACTERS

What important role did Emperor Wu of the Liang dynasty play in this period?

_____

_____

WHAT HAPPENED WHEN?

Tell what happened on each date.

304–439 CE _____

316 CE _____

317 CE _____

502 CE _____

WORD BANK

culture shock   inovice   passionate   edict

Complete each sentence with a word from the word bank.

1. A person who is just beginning the training to become a monk is called a _____.

2. If you were suddenly sent to live in a different country, you might suffer from _____.

3. An emperor might issue an _____ that the subjects must obey.

WITH A PARENT OR PARTNER

The chapter talks about waves of migration from north China to south China. With your parents or other adult family members or friends, discuss what it is like to migrate from one place to another, faraway place. In your history journal, write down how you and the other group members feel or would feel about such a move, and why.

CRITICAL THINKING

READING COMPREHENSION

1. What had the people from northern China lost when they left their former homes?

_____

2. What problems did the migrants face in south China?

_____

DRAWING CONCLUSIONS

Use the following chart to explain why Buddhism appealed to many Chinese people at this time. For each problem faced by the Chinese, explain how belief in Buddhism helped make it better. Then answer the question below in complete sentences.

Problem	How Buddhism Helped
1. People were worn out from constant warfare and oppression.	
2. People were abandoned by their government and other institutions.	
3. Women had stressful lives.	
4. The present life seemed to be an unending, useless struggle.	

How did Emperor Wu, who had converted to Buddhism, put Buddhist principles into action in government?

_____

_____

_____

GROUP TOGETHER

Wouldn't it be interesting to talk to other students about the rise of Buddhism after the Han dynasty? How was it a help to the Chinese people? What do you know about Buddhism today? Get a few friends together and ask your teacher to help you organize a discussion group at school. Have one person take notes and another person present the group's ideas to the class.

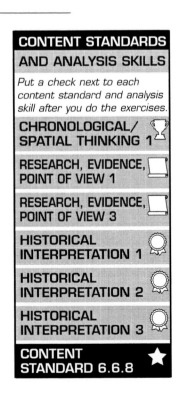

EPILOGUE

LEARNING OBJECTIVES

This chapter addresses Content Standard 6.6.2. It also addresses the following historical and social sciences analysis skills: Chronological and Spatial Thinking 1; Research, Evidence, and Point of View 3; Historical Interpretation 1. A complete list of content standards and analysis skills appears on pages 61–62 of this study guide.

CHAPTER SUMMARY

In 1986, some factory workers from Sichuan province stumbled upon an archaeological site that was completely unexpected. Unfortunately, the Three Gorges Dam, currently under construction along the Yangzi River, threatens many archaeological sites both known and unknown, as well as several species of endangered animals and more than a thousand cities and villages.

ACCESS

One way to look at human history is to see a cycle of growth, decline, and rebirth. One city exists for hundreds of years, and is then destroyed. Some time later, another group of people builds a new city on the same site, and the cycle starts again. This sometimes makes studying the ancient past difficult, because artifacts are destroyed by new construction. This chapter discusses the tug between archaeologists who want to study the artifacts and governments who want to develop land for their own purposes. In your history journal, answer the following question: Is it more important to know a people's history or help modern people live better lives? When you have finished the chapter, revisit your answer to see if your opinion remains the same.

WHAT HAPPENED WHEN?

Tell what happened on each date.

1986 _____

1994 _____

WORD BANK

gold leaf   gorges   eerie   intrigued

Complete each sentence with a word from the word bank.

1. The Yangzi River has cut deep _____ along its path.

2. To make plain metal more beautiful, you can coat it with _____.

3. Something that is scary-looking could be called _____.

WORD PLAY

The word *intrigued* can have different meanings depending on what part of speech it is used as. Use a dictionary to find out the different meanings of the word. Then write a new sentence for each meaning of the word.

_____

_____

_____

CRITICAL THINKING
ANALYZING POINT OF VIEW

1. Use the following chart to analyze the arguments of the two sides of the important issue discussed in this chapter: How to deal with ancient artifacts that are in the path of modern development. Write the arguments that each side would use, or the things that concern them the most. Then answer the question, using complete sentences.

Archaeologists and Historians	Chinese Government

2. Do you think there is a way to satisfy both sides of this argument? If so, explain what you think the solution is. If not, explain why you think so.

_____

_____

_____

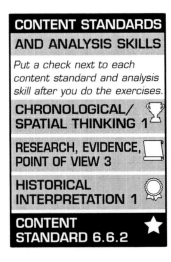

CONTENT STANDARDS AND ANALYSIS SKILLS

Put a check next to each content standard and analysis skill after you do the exercises.

CHRONOLOGICAL/ SPATIAL THINKING 1

RESEARCH, EVIDENCE, POINT OF VIEW 3

HISTORICAL INTERPRETATION 1

CONTENT STANDARD 6.6.2

Congratulations! Now that you have completed all the exercises, you have done important work to address the content standards for the ancient Chinese world. You have also practiced many valuable historical and social sciences analysis skills. Fill out this chart to keep a score of your knowledge and skills. The standards are described in full. Below each one you'll find icons with the chapter numbers inside them. Match these up with the checklists in each chapter by filling them in or checking them off.

GRADES SIX AND SEVEN HISTORY–SOCIAL SCIENCE CONTENT STANDARDS

6.1.1. Describe the hunter-gatherer societies, including the development of tools and the use of fire.

⭐ 1

6.1.3. Discuss the climatic changes and human modifications of the physical environment that gave rise to the domestication of plants and animals and new sources of clothing and shelter.

⭐ 2

6.6.1. Locate and describe the origins of Chinese civilization in the Huang-He [Yellow River] Valley during the Shang Dynasty.

⭐ intro ⭐ 3 ⭐ 4 ⭐ 5 ⭐ 6 ⭐ 12

6.6.2. Explain the geographic features of China that made governance and the spread of ideas and goods difficult and served to isolate the country from the rest of the world.

⭐ 1 ⭐ 12 ⭐ 15 ⭐ 20 ⭐ epi

6.6.3. Know about the life of Confucius and the fundamental teachings of Confucianism and Taoism.

⭐ 7 ⭐ 10 ⭐ 11 ⭐ 18 ⭐ 19

6.6.4. Identify the political and cultural problems prevalent in the time of Confucius and how he sought to solve them.

⭐ 7 ⭐ 8 ⭐ 9 ⭐ 10

6.6.5 .List the policies and achievements of the emperor Shi Huangdi in unifying northern China under the Qin Dynasty.

⭐ 13 ⭐ 15

6.6.6. Detail the political contributions of the Han Dynasty to the development of the imperial bureaucratic state and the expansion of the empire.

⭐ 14 ⭐ 15 ⭐ 16 ⭐ 17 ⭐ 18 ⭐ 21

6.6.7. Cite the significance of the trans-Eurasian "silk roads" in the period of the Han Dynasty and Roman Empire and their locations.

⭐ 20

6.6.8. Describe the diffusion of Buddhism northward to China during the Han Dynasty.

⭐ 20 ⭐ 22 ⭐ 23

1. Students explain how major events are related to one another in time.

2. Students construct various time lines of key events, people, and periods of the historical era they are studying.

3. Students use a variety of maps and documents to identify physical and cultural features of neighborhoods, cities, states, and countries and to explain the historical migration of people, expansion and disintegration of empires, and the growth of economic systems.

RESEARCH, EVIDENCE, AND POINT OF VIEW

1. Students frame questions that can be answered by historical study and research.

2. Students distinguish fact from opinion in historical narratives and stories.

3. Students distinguish relevant from irrelevant information, essential from incidental information, and verifiable from unverifiable information in historical narratives and stories.

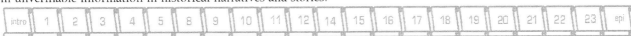

4. Students assess the credibility of primary and secondary sources and draw sound conclusions from them.

5. Students detect the different historical points of view on historical events and determine the context in which the historical statements were made (the questions asked, sources used, author's perspectives).

HISTORICAL INTERPRETATION

1. Students explain the central issues and problems from the past, placing people and events in a matrix of time and place.

2. Students understand and distinguish cause, effect, sequence, and correlation in historical events, including the long-and short-term causal relations.

3. Students explain the sources of historical continuity and how the combination of ideas and events explains the emergence of new patterns.

4. Students recognize the role of chance, oversight, and error in history.

5. Students recognize that interpretations of history are subject to change as new information is uncovered.

6. Students interpret basic indicators of economic performance and conduct cost-benefit analyses of economic and political issues.

REPORTS AND SPECIAL PROJECTS

There's always more to find out about ancient China. Take a look at the Further Reading and Websites section at the end of the book (pages 161–164). Here you'll find a number of books and online sources for different topics relating to ancient Chinese history and culture. Many of them will be available in your school or local public library.

GETTING STARTED

Explore the Further Reading section for any of these reasons.

— You're curious and want to learn more about a particular topic.

— You want to do a research report on ancient China.

— You still have questions about something covered in the book.

— You need more information for a special classroom project.

What's the best way to find the books that will help you the most?

LOOK AT THE SUBHEADS

The books are organized by topic. The subhead Religion tells you where to find books on ancient Chinese religious beliefs, for example. Go to Warfare to learn more about Sun-tzu and his ideas on war. Let the subheads give you ideas for reports and special projects.

LOOK AT THE BOOK TITLES

The titles of the books can tell you a lot about what's inside. The books listed under Philosophy offer modern translations of ancient Chinese philosophy texts.

LOOK FOR GENERAL REFERENCES

This section also lists general books, which are useful starting points for further research. General Works on Ancient China lists titles that provide a broad overview of ancient Chinese history. Judge by the titles which books will be the most useful to you. Other references include:

— Dictionaries

— Encyclopedias

— Atlases

OTHER RESOURCES

Information comes in all kinds of formats. Use the book to learn about primary sources. Go to the library for videos, DVDs, and audio materials. And don't forget about the Internet!

AUDIO-VISUAL MATERIALS

Your school or local library can offer documentary videos and DVDs on ancient China, as well as audio materials. If you have access to a computer, explore the sites listed in the Websites section of Further Reading and Websites (pages 163–164) for some good jumping-off points. These are arranged in alphabetical order, with brief descriptions of what you'll find on each site. Many websites list additional reading, as well as other Internet links you can visit.

What you've learned about the ancient Chinese world so far is just a beginning. Learning more is an ongoing adventure!

NAME _____

LIBRARY / MEDIA CENTER RESEARCH LOG

DUE DATE _____

Brainstorm: Other Sources and Places to Look

Places I **Know** to Look

What I Need to **Find**

I need to use:
- ☐ primary
- ☐ secondary

sources.

WHAT I FOUND

Title/Author/Location (call # or URL)

How I Found it

	Suggestion	Library Catalog	Browsing	Internet Search	Web link

Primary Source	Secondary Source

Book/Periodical	Website	Other

Rate each source from 1 (low) to 4 (high) in the categories below

helpful	relevant